Computer Security and Telerobotics for Everyone

By

Eamon P. Doherty Ph.D.
Co-authors: Gary Stephenson and Joel Fernandes

authorHOUSE™

1663 LIBERTY DRIVE, SUITE 200
BLOOMINGTON, INDIANA 47403
(800) 839-8640
WWW.AUTHORHOUSE.COM

First published by AuthorHouse 11/14/05

ISBN: 1-4208-9682-2 (sc)

Printed in the United States of America
Bloomington, Indiana

This book is printed on acid-free paper.

Dedication

This book is dedicated to **Dr. Chris Bloor,** of the University of Sunderland and his doctoral student **Paul Gnanayutham** for using robotics to help disabled people in England, India, and the United States. The book is also dedicated to **Jeff Marsh, Walter Engel, and Bruce Davis** who have tested both robots and telerobotics without pay to help disabled people. Lastly I wish to dedicate the book to my mom for all her support.

Acknowledgment

I would like to acknowledge all the students over the years who have worked with telerobotics, robots, and phones for helping disabled persons feed themselves, calling for help, and trying to do some activities of daily living. I would like to especially thank Joel Fernandes and coauthor Gary Stephenson for their works.

Disclaimer

This book represents my personal opinions and not those of Fairlieigh Dickinson University. My personal opinions do not represent those of anyone or group whom I have a contract with. These personal opinions do not represent the opinions of any committee do I belong to. I was not paid to endorse any products and the products I mention are only mentioned to give examples of them for personal use. I have not tried all products of related types but just picked inexpensive common items I could afford with my own pay. This is not a security manual but a book to teach concepts. It is best to seek the help of security professionals when one has digital assets that could be potentially accessed by a network.

My comments are personal thoughts and any views are not meant to criticize any particular products or people. My opinions are personal and do not represent official opinions for any committee or organization I belong to.

Table of Contents

Chapter 1 –
Introduction to Network Security and Physical Security

1.0 – Introduction to Network Security

I was teaching an introductory to network security class some years back that consisted of mostly graduate students and a few undergraduate seniors who were given permission to take the class. I would estimate that 90% of the class also consisted of people from developing nations and their outlook of technology and network security seemed to be greatly shaped by television and American movies. I asked this class in earnest what network security was. One young man from a developing nation said it was getting on the computer and typing in codes and using tools and matching wits live with a hacker trying to break in your system much like the 1980s movie "War Games". Another man echoed the same sentiment and spoke of a military officer on the TV show JAG who was typing in codes on the computer that was connected to a network in order to stop some catastrophic event. The class became very animated and it seemed clear that Hollywood created movies that allowed many viewers to perceive a distorted idea about network security. The above events are a small part of network security that a minority of professionals may face once in their career. It is not the norm.

The class I taught was vocal in their disappointment when they learned that a big part of network security was developing and enforcing policies such as computer usage, Internet usage, telephone usage (modems can connect to computers via phone), and the employee handbook. Without the proper legal policies, it would be difficult to prosecute any infractions done on the network because there would be few rules to break. I also explained that network security included physical security to keep the computers connected to the network, safe from people off the street or from other departments in a company who had no reason or authorization to access that computer on the network. I also explained that such mundane tasks like backing up data and restoring it, is critical to network security. Then I mentioned firewalls were necessary to keep various types of data and unauthorized users out. I mentioned access control devices such as passwords, usernames, and thumbprint (biometric) readers to limit the network to authorized users. Then I explained to the class that we would also study the need to update software, use antivirus software, perform vulnerability tests, and create a security plan to address all the issues concerning the network access and security of data and equipment. The class got a reality check when I finished with the need to screen employees and educate them in principles of information security.

1.1 – Introduction to Physical Security

The most secure system with firewalls and intrusion detection systems are worthless if someone can walk in and put in a disk or USB drive and collect what they want and leave. It is our opinion that physical security is considered by many computer scientists to be some type of low tech measures that are not worthy of consideration but in reality, any measure that protects the network is worthy of consideration. Physical security consists of locks for doors, cabling devices for tables, close circuit television, security guards, controlled access points, smoke alarms, intrusion detection systems, and proper policies and education.

1.2 – Locks and Cables

You might be surprised to learn that many people will have a computer in their home with a network connection in a room that has a door with no lock. These same people may be cutting their lawn and have the garage door up. It would be easy for a cyber thief to wait while you were cutting the lawn, walk in, and access your documents or purchase things online pretending to be you. This can be easy to do because many people have dial up modems or cable modems with the username and password saved. They may also have everything saved for quick purchases of books at places such as Amazon books.

In many institutions, we will see a resident's computer in a room with the door left often all day while the resident is away. Someone visiting another resident or a worker could just walk away with the computer, a monitor, or just access the Internet and perhaps download child pornography that could lead to a police investigation and possible arrests.

It is therefore important to have locks on the door to rooms with computers in private residences. Locks may have combinations of numbers or a key. It may not be possible to lock doors in an institution because cleaning people, dietitians, therapists, nurses, and doctors may need access to charts, the room, or the resident. The institutional computer user then needs stronger access controls and cabling and locks for the computer. One can purchase a cable and lock that looks like a bicycle lock and cable. Some computer tables will have a metal fastener or hole where the cable can be threaded and many desktop computers have metal rings built in them that allow a cable to go through.

Many institutional residents told me they do not want a laptop because it is too easy for someone to walk away with. They would rather have a large heavy desktop that is difficult to move and its movement would be questioned by the staff and the physical security personnel. However; that idea has been changing because some residents can put their laptop in a piece of furniture with lockable drawers that both saves space and conceals the laptop most of the time.

A bedridden man who was very worried about his computer getting stolen got web TV and told me that all he ever used it for was Internet surfing and email. Web TV was ideal for him because he only needed a special modem and a wireless keyboard and mouse. He told me that he left them out because nobody would steal them since keyboards can be as cheap as 5 US dollars now and the idea of being caught stealing a large nearly worthless item was too risky.

You need to select the cables and locks that are compatible with the equipment, polices, and lifestyle of your private residence or long term care facility. You should think about how easy it is to steal the equipment or for someone to gain unauthorized access to the machine while you are not there. You may start to get the idea that much of security is simply common sense, like taking preventative measures to ensure cyber crime is made unattractive to those who may want to engage in it to compromise your computer and network access.

1.3 – Smoke Alarms / Intrusion Alarms

Someone could easily break in the home and steal a computer as well as your personal art work, coins, and intellectual property on CDs. Therefore if one can afford it, it may be a good idea to get a burglar alarm and a service such as ADT that will monitor your home. Some of the alarm services also have smoke detection and carbon monoxide detection which is important because while smoke can be seen, carbon monoxide is invisible.

Imagine you are sitting at the computer and using the Internet early in the morning. You could have a furnace malfunction or a spouse start the car in a garage for a prolonged period of time in the winter, and the carbon monoxide would make you very sick and possibly cause you to faint. It is my personal opinion that smoke alarms, carbon monoxide alarms, and intrusion detection alarms are a good addition to the home. A combination smoke alarm and carbon monoxide alarm can be seen in Figure 1.1 below.

Figure 1.1 – Carbon Monoxide and Smoke Alarm

1.4 – Physical Security and Laptops

One time at the airport in Newark, I was carrying a laptop and asked the airline employee where the toilet was. He told me where it was and explained that many people put the laptop on the ground while using the toilet. There have been times where thieves will wait until a person is using the toilet and has the laptop on the ground. The thief will reach under the stall and grab the laptop and run away. The person will either be unaware the event happened or not be in a position to pursue the thief. Consequently, many people have purchased proximity detectors: where one unit goes in the person's pocket and one is placed inside the laptop. A hundred decibel siren will be audible if the unit gets more than 30 feet from the laptop owner with the other piece of equipment. Most people will drop a 100 decibel screeching object and run thereby allowing the owner to determine where the item is and obtain it when circumstances permit.

Many people are now asking themselves if they really need to carry a laptop that could be stolen in a hotel by cleaning people or at the airport. If they only need to check their email or a company website why not just use web TV at a hotel or a personal Blackberry device with web access and email. I once stayed in Las Vegas at the Monte Carlo Hotel and my room had a large television and web TV. Web TV is a system that consists of a modem and wireless keyboard and a mouse emulator that allows the user to surf the Internet and use a web based email system. I found web TV easy to use on a large screen television and many travelers find it sufficient to answer email and check a web based email system such as hotmail, earthlink, or America Online. Why carry a bulky and expensive laptop if your hotel has Web TV or you can get a cell phone or Blackberry device with email and Internet service?

Another service one can get is Cyber Angel. You must purchase some software, install it, and pay a yearly fee to the company for the Cyber Angel product. If the laptop is stolen, you let them know. Then when the thief connects the stolen unit to the Internet, the IP and location will be reported to Cyber Angel. The Cyber Angel incident response team will call the police in the appropriate jurisdiction and the laptop can be returned to the owner. It is an excellent idea.

1.5 – Controlled Entry / Exit Points / Closed Circuit TV
It is very well known in the United States that shoplifting and theft costs merchants approximately a minimum of one million dollars per day. The more entry and exit points, generally the more theft that exists. Many nursing homes and hospitals have increased physical security because of increased regulations in information security due to the HIPAA Act of 1996 that was instituted by President Bill Clinton. This increased physical security sometimes results in a single access point for visitors to enter and exit. This point often has security guards who use closed circuit television around the facility to monitor theft, violence, potential sexual harassment, and people accessing restricted areas.

As a volunteer at a nursing home I am aware that certain institutions may store radio active isotopes for treating cancers, legitimate drugs that may have a high street value, as well as confidential information that is protected by the HIPAA Act of 1996. I now understand why it is important that this increased security is needed so that someone off the street cannot come in and steal isotopes, or drugs, or access a computer connected to the network and download private health care information protected by HIPAA.

1.6 – Limiting Physical Access within an Organization
Sometimes, like on a very hot day, people will leave the back door open in a remote corner of a company and keep it propped open with a rock. This remote corner may be near some

woods or share a parking lot with another organization. In any case it leaves an invitation to intruders, and employees should be educated not to do this. Sometimes this is done to alleviate heat when a fan or air conditioner is not working. It may be done so that one can quickly exit for a smoke. It seems innocent enough but can have bad effects on security.

Bogus employees without an authorization badge will follow behind another authorized employee in the company, through to a restricted access area. The employee who follows may ask 'keep that door open, I am going through'. This is bad because the employee who follows may not have access to that area and if there is a problem, the access time and name will be listed as the first employee. It is important to educate employees of deceptions like this and to keep doors shut; or simply to ask the other person for their appropriate identification or authorization.

1.7 – Structure, Wiring, Dampness

It seems odd to think of these things as a security risks but a damp environment will cause your paper documents to get damp and grow mold and ruin the paper. Damp environments may accelerate rust in electronic equipment as well as cause failures. It is best to have someone check the humidity and then ask the computer manufacturer what an acceptable level of humidity is. If your room is too humid, a dehumidifier may be needed. A dehumidifier, as in figure 1.2, can be obtained at most appliance stores for about 220 US dollars.

Figure 1.2 – A Dehumidifier to Remove Dampness from the Air

Another important issue is that a home computer network may be set up in a house built in the early twentieth century, with the electrical service carried by knob and tube wiring. Often such wires are thin and not far from old dried out, exposed beams. People will often have a computer monitor, desktop computer, printer, fax machine, scanner, broad band modem, and router that are all plugged in. The result is that the wires are pulling too much amperage and getting hot. Having too many devices plugged in on old wiring can lead to a fire.

Many times people will have a home office for consulting that deals with computer technology and have a small network set up. People notice that technology frequently changes and they often needs to buy books, software and manuals to keep up. The consultant often has to keep all these books and equipment in case he or she has to go back and work on a previous project for a customer. The result is that the consultant has tons of equipment and books that stress the residence he or she lives in. The result is that the books can cause beams to warp, walls to sag, and can lead to a floor caving in if the wooden house is not properly structured. For peace of mind, two or three household fire extinguishers ought to placed (together with a battery operated torch) at strategic places throughout the home.

1.8 – Fire Suppression Systems

A fire suppression system is very important because a fire can quickly start and destroy property as well as life. Many residential homes have no fire suppression system and since they are wooden, they can quickly burn and destroy all the network equipment. Commercial buildings may have water sprinklers which are great for suppressing a fire but can damage paper documents, network equipment, and books. There also exist buildings with Halon gas fire suppression systems. I worked in such a building as a mainframe computer operator (IBM ES9000) many years ago and was told that the Halon gas will rapidly consume all oxygen and thus extinguish the fire. However; people must evacuate quickly too because oxygen is a key component to sustain human life.

There are class A, B, and C fire extinguishers. A person in the computer room should also be trained in the use of them and know which one to use for a paper fire or electrical fire. One person on each floor in the commercial building should also be trained as the fire marshal and it is his or her responsibility to tell workers where the fire exits are and where to line up outside during a fire drill. Each fire marshal should have a head count for the number of workers on each floor. The fire marshal may be responsible for evacuating everyone and should tell office workers where to stand until the fire rescue trucks arrive. The fire marshal may tell the fire rescue people that everyone is accounted for or that someone may still be inside and in need of rescue.

1.9 – Flooding, Storms, and Managing Risk

It is common knowledge that storms and floods devastate areas on a frequent basis. For example, Lincoln Park New Jersey frequently floods during heavy rains and a major flood occurs approximately every ten years. The flood is often so bad that the first floor of a house may get a few feet of water. Such flooding may completely ruin computers and network operations. We can see that there needs to be planning and budgeting for such disasters.

Let us now look at a formula for this situation that you ought to know for the general network security credential known as the SSCP, System Security Certified Professional.

The **ARO**, Annual Rate of Occurrence, is once every ten years 1/10 or .1

The **SLE**, Single Loss Exposure could be 100% all is ruined and that means 10 pieces of equipment at $1000 each, a $2000 piece of equipment and 50 hours labor at $50 per hour.

The **ALE**, The Annual Loss Expectancy = SLE * ARO

ALE = ARO (.1) * SLE (10* $1000 + $2000 + 50*$50.00)

ALE = .1 * $10,000 + $2000 + $2500

ALE = .1 * $14,500 = $1,450 per year.

The company should budget $1,450 per year toward the loss.

1.91 – Practical Example of Risk Management

Suppose John Iron-Horse donates a piece of great land to a costal town in South Carolina for a mini data center. The only real drawback is that a twister is known to pass through the area every 25 years. You are the town public administrator and need to show the insurance company that the new center is not a significant risk as John points out. The mini data center has a broadband modem worth $100, a desktop computer, printer, scanner, copier, and fax worth $2000.00, and a router worth $100 and an array of sensors worth $1000.00.

At a recent meeting, Ms. Jones pointed out that local weather records showed that there has been only 50% damage to most houses or business hit by such a twister and that is known as exposure factor, EF, and should be factored into the equation for the insurance company. Let us do the math for the insurance company now.

ARO = 1/25 or .04   EF = 50%   SLE = EF * Price of All Assets

ALE = ARO * SLE

ALE = .04 * .5 * ($100 + $2000 + $100 + $1000)

ALE = .02 * $3200 = $64.00

The town needs to budget $64.00 per year for risk on such computer and network equipment. Most people would consider that risk negligible and decide to self insure rather than pay to insure it. It is considered low risk.

Suppose there is another town meeting and a local company says they could build a cement room using a very dry mixture, for $1200. They said this is what is known in tornado protection terms as a safe room and they would guarantee nothing would be damaged.

The town administrator wonders if the $1200 investment will be worth it. First Plymouth Bank says they would finance the $1200 for $72 a year for 50 years. Then, after the 50 years they would continue to charge $72 a year for one of their customers to maintain and inspect the facility. So let us do the math.

ALE (Before) – ALE (After) – Annual Cost of Safeguard = Value of Safeguard
$64.00   -   0   - $72.00   = -$8.00

On a mathematical level it may not be worth adding the safeguard, but many people have pointed out that the weather patterns are changing due to global warming and the storms are becoming more frequent. The town administrator may decide the extra $8.00 is worth the piece of mind.

1.95 – Learning More about Topics Covered in This Chapter

The topics of managing risk and budgeting costs to insure a network is safe and secure against any natural disasters, equipment failure can be learned from reading the SSCP, Systems Security Practitioner Study Guide [1].

Suppose you are also interested in preparing your home or home-based business for disaster and creating a plan to deal with fire, hurricanes, nuclear power plant disasters, winter storms, tornadoes, and floods. You should consult an excellent easy to read book that is published by FEMA (Federal Emergency Management Agency) called, "Are You Ready" [2]. There are also classes taught at Fairleigh Dickinson University in the Master of Administrative Science program that deal with Network Security, Emergency Management, and Risk Management [3].

REFERENCES

1. Jacobs, J., Clemmer, L., Dalton, M., Posluns, J., (2003)," SSCP, Systems Security Practitioner Study Guide, Syngress Publishing, ISBN 1-931836-80-9, Page 265
2. FEMA, "Are You Ready?", FEMA, Washington D.C., H-34 September 1993,
3. URL http://sas.fdu.edu Visited July 19,2005

Chapter 2 –
Networks Then and Now in the USA

2.0 – Networks in the Old Days Influence Networks Today

The telegraph was the way to quickly send data across long distances in the United States during the American Civil War. It was as convenient as having text based email without the ability to send attachments. The American Civil War took place between 1861-1865. A picture of a telegraph key, which was part of such a system, can be seen in Figure 2.1. Each word was broken into Morse code which consisted of a dot which sounded like a dit or a dash which sounded like a long dah. There was of course a pause of silence between words and a smaller pause of silence between letters. There were basically two states and unused parts of this network were filled with silence to differentiate letters from words. These words or messages traveled around the United States on copper wire.

Thomas Alva Edison played no small part in advancing the telegraph from a simple form of human communication over very long distances across the American hinterland, to a commercial tool (the Tickertape) used on Wall Street to monitor fluctuations on the stock market. Edison is credited with having created a simple remote diagnostic tool for determining when a fault had occurred and rectifying it on-line.

An A in Morse Code is dit dah and today, computer users agree on a format that the letter A is made up of a certain group of two states, namely ones and zeroes. This standardization exists because a group of various interests in the United States formed the American Standard Code for Information Interchange (ASCII) in 1968 [1]. It was decided that A would be 64 hex or 0110 0010. Here we see a one or high state, 2.5 volts to 5.0 volts and a 0, or low state of about .5 volts to approximately 2 volts. Let us suppose some copper wires in the 1860s carried the letter A in a message from the Grand Army of the Republic Headquarters in the North to Fort Leavenworth, Kansas. A person tapping the line with a telegraph sounder would hear dit dah. Today, it is quite possible that in some rural parts of the United States those same copper wires could have been converted to phone lines and may carry tones simulating one state or another. When the packet gets to a switching station and then onto a fiber backbone, it will have to be digitized into 1s and 0s.

Figure 2.1 – Dr. Doherty using a Railroad Telegraph in Rural Upstate New York

Someone said to me they could not believe that during the Civil War the telegraph was almost an instant messaging capability. Many young people will think the 1860s and the telegraph are ancient history, but I say that we have a connection to the past. Let's examine this news story that the BBC carried in 2003 about the last Civil War Officer widow who just died nearly 140 years after the conflict. When the woman named Alberta Martin died in Alabama, she was still receiving a small pension [2]. Just imagine how far into the future we will be paying off compensation debts to people for current service. One should also remember that such an event as the Civil War is not entirely a closed historic book; not when the government was still paying off pensions to relatives of survivors as recently as 2003.

2.1 – The Telephone and Joining an Internet Service Provider
Many people in the United States including our secondary editor Jeff Marsh have a home computer, a modem and a telephone line. They double click on an icon that says Dial America Online or some other Internet Service Provider (ISP) and this starts a process that uses the dialer service in the operating system. The icon is an operating system shortcut that uses a dialing service in the computer. The operating system is configured with your telephone number and the telephone number of your ISP. When the icon is clicked, the operating system makes a system call and invokes the Telephone Application Interface (TAPI) and the operating system obtains the line and a call handle [3]. An Application Program Interface (API) called TAPI Request Call is passed the telephone number and it is stored in a buffer. The number is dialed and a connection is obtained. Some acoustic sounds are passed back and forth over the modem and a handshake or protocol connection is made. Then there is a brief time for the ISP to check the username stored in the buffer associated with the icon and the saved password too. This is known as the authentication process. If the username and password match for

that account, the user is then connected to the network such as America Online or whoever the ISP happens to be.

Modems usually work at speeds measured in Bits Per Second (bps). We talked earlier about bits (short for binary digits), as being either a high or low signal, or a 1 or 0. Modems are often rated at 14.4 Kbps or kilobits per second. Some are rated at 28 Kbps and others are reported to approach speeds of 56 Kbps but never reaching them. If you hear the term baud, just divide any number by 4 to get the 'bits per second' rate. Caution: If you throw that old computer out and that account is active and there is an internal modem, then someone can sign on as you. If the person goes and sends a threatening email to someone or an organization, this is Cyber terrorism [4]. It can be misconstrued as a violent crime that appears to be from you. Anytime someone pretends to be someone else, that is known as a masquerading attack [5]. Let us hope a Cyber crime investigator can clear your name if an investigation occurs. Such a situation is not the ISP's fault but the person's fault who saves their password in the machine and discards a machine with an active account. It is best to erase or destroy the hard drive before discarding a machine.

It is easy to get a dial up account for connecting to a private network or Internet. You can get a CD or diskette in the mail from an ISP such as Net Zero or America Online. You run the program and it asks for your phone number, and gives you an option for some dial up numbers in your area so you do not incur a long distance charge. Then you agree a number and a local destination for you to use. You will then choose a screen name / username and password and you are ready to be connected to a private network such as America Online which is a wonderful service with chat rooms for specialized interests such as sports cars or video games. If you choose, they have a portal where you can access the World Wide Web. Many people like the private network to public network concept. They also like the telephone support that the ISP provides which can be technical or may enable you to find something out about your individual account information.

2.2 – The Telephone Network, Copper Wires, Modern Networks

Many people believe that the telephone and telephone network is an invention of the twentieth century but it is not. The Patent 174465 was given to Alexander Graham Bell for the telephone in the year 1876. (Bell's name later became famously associated with Bell Labs and Ma Bell) This device let people talk great distances over electric wires. The principles were actually known since the 1840s but Bell made the first practical device. The archives show that in the year 1887 approximately 150,000 people had a telephone in the USA and about 7,000 people in Russia and 26,000 people in the UK. However; Signal Loss / Attenuation limited distance from Boston to Chicago. It is important to realize that the greater the distance is, the weaker the signal gets. That concept still holds true for both phone networks and Local Area Networks (LANs) today. That is why you need repeaters every 100 feet to retransmit the signal or an amplifier to boost it for your home or office local area network. However; the amplifier will also boost the noise too so it is better to retransmit it.

The telephones from the late 1800s and early 1900s had a hand crank magneto that was used to generate a charge. The user would crank the handle and lift the receiver and put it to one ear and speak to the operator. The operator would ask them where they wanted to be connected to and a series of manual circuit connections were made. You can see a late 1800s phone in figure 2.2. The hand crank is to the right of the mouthpiece where the user speaks into.

Figure 2.2 – 1890s Hand Cranked Telephone that Works between 2 Stations

Let's now examine Ohm's Law to understand the relationship of power, voltage, and current. Voice or signals carried over a copper wire. The signal strength is measured in watts according to Ohm's Law P (Watts) = E (Voltage) X I (current)

> **EXAMPLE :**   4 Watts   = 2 Volts x 2 Amps

Now we will think about attenuation in a scientific way. Attenuation is the loss of power over distance. The ratio of power increase or loss over various points in the wire is measured in decibels. The decibel is a metric that lets us compare two signal strengths. Power level one is our starting location and will be labeled as P1. Power level two or P2 is the level of power on the copper wire 200 feet away.

- dB = 10 X log 10 (P1 / P2)
- dB = 10 X log 10 (4 / 2)
- 3db = 10 X .3
-
- Every time the power doubles +3db
- Every time we lose half the power -3db

The thinner the wire, the higher gauge it is. Nineteen gauge, 19 AWG, is average wire. The signals lose decibel levels over distance. A person with a high frequency voice like pop star Michael Jackson would find his voice would be soaked up by a thin copper phone wire over a certain distance and not be heard. A person like Lurch on the Addams family movie would be heard with no problem on the same distance because he has a low frequency voice. The phone company used loading coils so a variety of peoples voices were heard easily but unfortunately this limited bandwidth to an effective range of 300 Hertz to 3300 Hertz though the phone company can use 0-4000 Hertz. There are 4000 cycles or sine waves a second that the phone company has available. Pulse code modulation can sample the line 8000 times a second (4000 X 2). The voice analog signal can therefore be digitally encoded with 8 bits per sampling encoded, 8000 in a second, to produce 64,000 bits per second, bps, on a DS-0 Channel [7].

People with regular phone lines ask me why their friends who order digital subscriber line service, commonly known as DSL, near a switching station have higher data rates. The longer the wire, the more attenuation or signal loss, that occurs and the less usable frequencies or bandwidth that is available. If we use more power on the wire so we can try to send more data further, the wire gets hotter and there is a danger of fire. When one also uses more power on a wire, the wire can act as an antenna and cause interference or allow eavesdropping more easily and thus security is compromised.

The same principles hold when you have a home network. The fatter the copper wire, the more power you can use and the more bandwidth you have. You will find coax cable or RG 58 can even allow you to carry 57 cable television channels and Internet service. If you set up a network in your house and have an electrician run the wires, he will not allow you to go more than 300 feet with certain gauge wires. They have a chart with coaxial cable, optical fiber, untwisted pair (UTP), twisted pair. Each set of wires is rated for a certain bandwidth and allows a certain transmission speed of data to reliably travel a certain distance with certain power requirements to stay within a safe operating temperature. Longer distances mean there is attenuation and there will be poor communications and too many requests to resend lost data packets. There are International Electrical and Electronic Engineers (IEEE) and International Standard Organization (ISO) standards that are on charts that network installation professionals adhere to [6].

In chapter 3 you will see how a research assistant and I used special Ethernet power line connectors to connect some computers together in the house using the existing copper electrical wires to carry data. In that experiment, one computer was connected to the Internet and all the computers were on the same Microsoft workgroup and thus part of the same network. The farther away we get from the main computer that was connected to the Internet, the slower the data rate was from other computers in the home that accessed the Internet. Everything has to do with bandwidth and attenuation. The goal of this little history lesson is to teach the physics of power, decibels, attenuation, and heat. The main lesson is that if you use fatter cables like RG8, like your cable TV cable, you have more bandwidth and faster transmission speeds.

2.1 – Why have a Home Network?

I will relate a story that shows the need for retaining old machines in a residential home that is used as both a home consulting office and a family residence. The father is a computer consultant who creates applications for a variety of customers throughout the world. Some customers use old machinery and operating systems while others have more modern personal computing equipment. The father gets a new computer every other year. Each son or daughter gives their machine to a younger sibling and gets a computer from the older sibling. Then those machines migrate to extended family as time goes on. Thus each family member upgrades every two years or gets a new computer. Everyone is happy and the landfills are not filled with their electronic equipment. I liked the idea when I heard it because it is an environmentally sound policy the father has adopted and allows various family members to get a new or better computer every two years without straining the family budget.

One of the family members told me it is good because if dad's client from his consulting business has an application that needs to be done in C++ version 6.0 on a Windows 95 platform, they can test it on that machine. No operating system emulators are needed and they will know right away if the software will work on the type of machine setup that the client has. The person went on to say many of the software licenses with the installation key are lost and they cannot reinstall that software on another machine. I learned that keeping the old machines makes both good environmental sense as well as good business sense.

I have increased my own interests in network security and computer forensics and found it useful to keep my old computers with Windows 3.1, 95, 98, and Windows XP to examine various aspects of the file systems and operating systems. I am an inventor too and may sometimes want to make something in Windows 98 using Visual C++ 6.0 and send it to my newer machine upstairs with Windows XP Home Edition to see how it works on other operating systems. The family I mentioned above and I have both found that we can have an intranet in our homes if those machines use the Ethernet power line adapters on the internal wiring in the house. That means a network within the home that has no computers connected to the Internet. Since the machines are not connected to the Internet and do not use email, surf the Internet, or get files from outside the house, they are relatively safe because no malware (malicious-software) gets introduced. The computers with Windows 95, 3.1, and 98 operating systems do not need any special firewalls, software updates, or other security devices that machines which are connected to the Internet need. These machines are only connected to each other in the house and never venture on any other public networks.

I live in a beautiful old home and the thought of drilling holes and running wires is unbearable. I chose not to use wireless connectivity because it was my opinion that the machine with Windows version 3.1 could not connect to wireless equipment easily or be a safe member of the network. However; someone could connect to my intranet network if they trespassed on my property, came up to my outside outlet with their laptop and Ethernet power line adapter, and plugged it in. Caution: Remember to lock the access to the outdoor outlet because it is a vulnerability that can be exploited. Now you are starting to understand network security.

Whatever you do, there is always something a determined hacker or criminal may try to do to penetrate the network. You always need to think a step ahead, and be on your guard.

I found that my Intranet was fairly easy to set up by creating a common workgroup on each MS Windows 95/98/XP machine and using the Ethernet power line adapters that connect to each computer as well as the electrical sockets. Then the wiring in the house allows every machine to be connected to every other machine. It is an instant mesh topology that is very robust. Each Ethernet power line network adapter cost me approximately 50 US Dollars (USD) and can be purchased at places such as Comp USA. Belkin and about 14 other companies create these adapters and they are all interchangeable because they use a common standard that is adhered to for Ethernet power line adapters. A picture of such an adapter is in Figure 2.3.

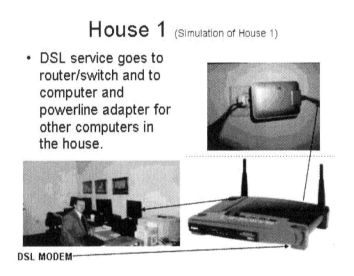

Figure 2.3 – The Ethernet Power Line Adapter in the Network

It is easy to connect another computer if your computer has an RJ45 connector and built in Local Area Network(LAN) card like my Hitachi Pentium 133 MHz with Windows 95. Otherwise you have to buy an external USB wireless card or get an Ethernet Adapter for your PCMCIA slot. Perhaps you want to use power line adapters or a telephone line adapter to use the internal wiring of your house. Maybe you want to run your own wiring. You may even want to use wireless networking. You now have 4 possibilities medias for connecting computers. Some machines may have Windows 98 while others have XP or Windows 95 or Windows ME.

In any case the wizards for creating a network in Microsoft Windows are fairly easy to use and please use the help screen to name a workgroup. There is also an absolutely fascinating book that is easy to read for the beginner and computer network professional alike and discusses step by step how to set these up and the pros and con of each setup such as power line adapters, wireless, etc... I must confess that the authors of the book and myself are both great fans of Linksys equipment for both its simplicity and low price. The book is called the Linksys Networks, The Official Guide, Second Edition. It is written by Kathy Ivens and Larry Seltzer. The book is published by the Osborne Group of McGraw Hill and the ISBN is 0-07-223072-X.

REFERENCES

1. Moulton, P.,(2001)"The Telecommunication Survival Guide", Prentice Hall Publishing, Upper Saddle River, N.J., Page 182-189

2. Last Civil War Widow – URL Visited July 19,2005
    http://news.bbc.uk/1/hi/world/americas/2677095.stm

3. Grigonis, R.,(2000),"Computer Telephony Encyclopedia", Published by CMP Books, ISBN 1-57820-045-8, Pages 392-3

4. Shinder, D., Tittel, E., (2002)"Scene of the Cybercrime, Computer Forensics Handbook, Rockland, MA, ISBN 1-931836-65-5, Page 19

5. Maiwald, E., (2001),"Network Security, A Beginner's Guide", Osborne – McGraw Hill Publishing, Berkeley, California, ISBN 0-07-213324, Page 25

6. Moulton, P.,(2001)"The Telecommunication Survival Guide", Prentice Hall Publishing, Upper Saddle River, N.J., Page 310-321

7. Moulton, " ", Page 59-60

Chapter 3 –
Industrial Espionage and Violating Intellectual Property

3.1 – Introduction to Industrial Espionage

The thought of espionage and the leaking of secret information may bring back the image of old black and white movies and characters lurking in smoke filled bars in the bad side of town. It may seem something distant and not relevant to what you need to know. However; the violation of trade secrets could be done by a person who may not consciously ever intend to do such a thing. Suppose you live in a place with a high cost of living such as New Jersey. You are young and planning to purchase a house and get married and live in a nice suburb. Suppose you are a bit ambitious and wish to move on to the next higher paying job that will allow you to pay for that wedding and put a down payment on a home. You then look on the Internet and see a job posted for a biometric device just like the one you work on and contact that person on a hotmail or yahoo account. The account may look okay because the account name appears temporary and job related.

Unbeknownst to you, the person who placed the advert calls you on a cell phone that was paid for in cash from a convenience store and is virtually untraceable. They use a calling card that they paid cash for from the convenience store. The person went to a convenience store that has a high turnover of employees and a high traffic of customers. The caller says he is from company xyz and will be in your area tomorrow. You meet at a restaurant for the interview. He is there early in his new suit. His car is parked around the corner. He is very pleasant and tells you about how great your life at the company will be and how much money you will make. You have a great meal and he picks up the bill with cash. During the meal he tells you he has been in some trouble with his boss because he is too nice and has hired some dead wood who were not qualified for the job. You sympathize and want to show you are certainly not dead wood. You tell him all about the romulation device in detail showing how smart you are.

He says how wonderful you did in the interview and has all the detailed notes from your interview showing how competent you are. He will run it by his boss and get back to you. Some time goes by and there is no news of the job. The cell phone he called you on is out of service. The email account is bouncing back your email. The company he told you he is with doesn't exist or does not have an office where he said. Your current boss informs you there is a new computer network device almost exactly the same as the romulator on the Internet for half the price from a country that has a poor working relationship with the USA. The above case illustrates how a dubious person eager to move ahead by changing jobs might commit industrial espionage. This is a dramatization of the concept but it shows how easily a person can be duped and the consequences for the entire company where that person is presently employed.

We will now examine in this chapter how the Ethernet power line network adapters could be misused by examining the Insider threat. A screwdriver for example can be a tool used to build a wheelchair for someone in need or it can be a burglar tool. It depends on the user and context. The same can be said about computer networks and components.

The previous example showed how somebody innocent, who is trying to get ahead, could easily be duped by someone. Later in this chapter we will discuss the insider threat and how someone could use Ethernet power line adapters for establishing a covert network inside a company or research facility and sending the information to a person on the outside. We will also examine the motivations for such behavior. I took a class on network security at Fairleigh Dickinson University in the School of Administrative Science and learnt that it is often a company's current and former employees who are the biggest security risk.

Chapter 4 will examine some of the countermeasures a company can use such as screening potential employees with background searches and establishing a system of clearances for sensitive data. Such systems are used by employers in the defense industry as well as by research and development divisions for some telecommunication companies.

Economic Espionage is defined by Title 18 of United States Code Section 1831 as "whoever knowingly performs targeting or acquisition of trade secrets to knowingly benefit any foreign government, foreign instrumentality, or foreign agent." The theft of trade secrets is covered by Title 18 United States Code 1832. and is "whoever knowingly performs targeting or acquisition of trade secrets to convert a trade secret to knowingly benefit anyone other than the owner."

According to literature distributed in cooperation between the Federal Bureau of Investigation (FBI) and the United States Department of Justice, the trade secret can be "all forms of financial, business, scientific, technical, economic or engineering information, including plans, compilations, program devices, formulas, designs, prototypes, methods, techniques, processes, procedures, programs, or codes intangible, and whether or how stored, compiled, or memorialized physically, electronically, graphically or in writing, which the owner has taken reasonable measures to protect; and has independent economic value." The literature further states that this is "commonly referred to as classified proprietary information or trade information."

We now know what constitutes a trade secret and the laws protecting it and we know a simple motivation one might have to disclose it. Now the rest of this chapter will examine the technical aspects of how trade secrets could leak in a facility with firewalls and what one would consider adequate security. The rest of this chapter is an excerpt of a paper that was included in the proceeding of the Department of Homeland Security Conference in Boston, Massachusetts from April 26-28 at the Trade Center. Permission was given for the paper to be published outside that conference. The authors and coauthor of the following paper are Dr. Eamon P. Doherty and a Fairleigh Dickinson University MAS student named Sean Boero. The only adaptation that has been done to the paper is to put a prefix of three before the figure number in order to coincide with our chapter numbers.

Addressing the Insider Threat from Unauthorized Area Networks

ABSTRACT: The problem of covert unauthorized networks within a school, government office, or business posses a significant security problem in the United States, and with its territories and allies. Such networks can inexpensively be set up by people with minimal technical skills. These networks can also be the source of large losses of sensitive documents and revenue due to the security leaks of trade secrets. These unauthorized networks may also allow communication and collaboration between groups on different floors in the building who may piece together a secret project. This paper also examines how a company with expensive enterprise firewalls and a full security staff also needs to develop a strategy to monitor the voltage on various electrical power lines within the facility by using various pieces of electronic equipment to detect covert data transmissions. This paper demonstrates how easy it is to use a laptop, an extra network card, a few Ethernet power line adapters strategically placed in a home based business or organization, and a wireless access point can create an undetected network inside the facility that can be broadcast offsite. This paper will examine strategies to monitor power lines, check for covert unauthorized area networks, and establishing an incident response policy and team to handle such security breaches.

Introduction to the Insider Threat: The insider threat of an unauthorized area network in a research facility, business, or the home can be the result of carelessness or a deliberate effort. Let us first look at how an unauthorized area network could happen by accident. First of all, the laptops often come with wireless cards in addition to Ethernet connectors. If the wireless connections are enabled and Microsoft Windows is used with the default workgroup name, it is certainly possible for the shared documents to be accessible on various machines and potentially someone with a laptop, wireless connection, and a directional antenna, such as the Cantenna, might be able to access the shared documents area from outside the building in a parking lot. A person who is in a hurry could drop a document in the shared documents instead of the "My Documents" folder allowing unwanted sharing. A person who was not paying attention could right click on the drive and enable sharing and after one more selection, that drive and its contents could be shared.

The insider threat can also be from a planned effort by people who wish to pilfer trade secrets from the organization and work covertly and collaboratively on pieces of the project to assemble the larger project. People in a facility could unplug their cable from the computer and put it in an Ethernet power line adapter and plug it in the wall to use the wiring within the wall to transmit data throughout the building. They could use a pre-designated workgroup name and the shared documents folder. This network would be off the grid so to speak and would not be known to the network administrators. It would also mean the large enterprise security firewalls would be bypassed.

In certain circumstances, Internet could be available in this setup too. If there was a wireless router switch connected to the power lines by an Ethernet power line adapter. That connectivity may be extended to the parking lot or across the street.

The Experiment

Many businesses are in houses that were former residences. We wished to determine the quality of the connectivity within a house and examine the feasibility of an unauthorized area network. We bought 2 Ethernet power line adapters as shown in figure 1 and connected to them to a desktop and laptop within a house. The desktop was connected to a DSL line as well as an Ethernet power line adapter. We moved the laptop to different floors in the house as well as outside and we plugged the Ethernet power line adapter in the wall. The experiment concluded with visits to neighbor's homes to see if connectivity was possible from their outlets.

We wished to investigate what kind of data rates would be available within a house to get an idea of the size of the documents that could be passed around the house. We also wished to examine the quality of the Internet connection by accessing the same Internet URL and obtaining a metric on the data rate to our machines.

Legal Aspects of the Experiment

It is noteworthy that an institutional review board (IRB) at Prof. Doherty's university approved the work and all parties involved in the research signed informed consents and were debriefed after the research. Any risks were accepted by the participants.

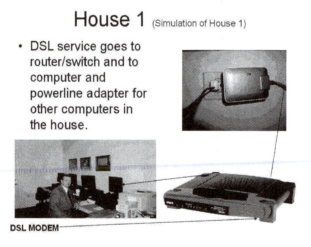

FIGURE 3.1 - Ethernet Power Line Adapter

Equipment Used

- Belkin Powerline Ethernet Adapter
- (Model F5D4070C4802076),
- Gateway Desktop Computer
- (Model 7310S).,
- Belkin software, CAT 5 ether- net patch cables
- Linksys / Router Switch
- Laptop Computer

Within House 1 – Outlet 1
40" Away

- Checked for download speed at www.pcpitstop.com

- Laptop received a reported download speed of 1924Kbps

- Gateway Laptop (Model ARC200),

Simulated picture of testing

Figure 3.2 – Testing the Connection from 40 Inches Away

Results

We can see in figure two that from a distance of forty inches away, the data rate was fairly good at 1924 kilobits per second. This was acceptable for passing low resolution pictures and text based documents of considerable size.

House 1 – 60 Feet Away
Same Floor

- Plugged the Ethernet
- Powerline Adapter directly into a electrical outlet in the room, located approximately 60' away from the other outlet and located on the same floor.

- Connectivity was established. Checked for download speed at www.pcpitstop.com and received a reported download speed of **1204 Kbps**.

Simulated picture of testing

Figure 3.3 – Sixty Feet Away Same Floor

We can see in figure three that from a distance of sixty feet away, the data rate was fairly good at 1204 kilobits per second but the same distance going upstairs was half the data rate. Both locations were considered acceptable for passing low resolution pictures and text based documents of considerable size.

House 1 – Outlet is 60 feet away from source (upstairs- 512 Kbps)

- Checked for download speed at www.pcpitstop.com and received a reported download speed of 512 Kbps.

Simulated picture of testing

Figure 3.4 – Sixty Feet Away Upstairs

House 1 – Outside Outlet (Rear Deck) 1979 Kbps

- Plugged the Ethernet Powerline Adapter directly into an available electrical outlet outside of the home in the rear deck area approximately 25' from the other outlet. Connectivity was established.

- Checked for download speed at www.pcpitstop.com and received a reported download speed of 1979 Kbps.

Simulation of Ethernet Powerline Adapter in outlet at site.

Figure 3.5 – Connectivity from an Outside Outlet

The Insider Outsider Connectivity

We have already established that insider connectivity and unauthorized collaboration can happen within the facility. However; you may now be wondering how such data can be passed innocuously to the outside. Perhaps 2.4 GHz signals are monitored or perhaps there are even jamming devices to prevent wireless transmission. Many houses and businesses have outside outlets that are used to operate outdoor electric equipment such as weed whackers, shrub trimmers, and other lawn care equipment. The outsider could easily be disguised as a lawn care company and plug into an outlet. Many landscapers and lawn care specialists also use computers to keep track of visits, billing, and chemicals placed on the lawn. Connectivity to the Internet would not be suspicious because a lawn care specialist may need to connect to a website concerning OSHA standards regarding exposure to various pesticides.

The outside outlet in our experiment gave a data rate of 1979 Kilobits per second. This is certainly a high enough data rate to pass large text based documents with pictures or massive documents with pictures provided they are in a pdf format which is common for various government documents. Pdf is a format that is considered very efficient and is created by Adobe. Such formats allow the transmissions of large documents where bandwidth is limited.

Motivations for Spying

There may be various reasons for the insider threat. There could be a rival company or foreign government that offers a large amount of cash for secret documents. People who have excessive debt may be vulnerable to compromise. Some of the reasons for excessive debt beyond a person's control could be due to: children selecting a college above the family's ability to pay, a spouse with an alcohol or substance abuse problem, or a spouse who uses credit to live beyond the means of the family.

It would best to consult a law enforcement professional and psychologist to determine other types of motivations for spying and then try to incorporate their opinions into the vulnerability assessment of the corporation. Perhaps better screening of potential employees or periodic interviews with employees could reveal a potential threat. It would be common sense to believe that intervention before an event is less costly than a response.

Incident Response Policy and Teams

It is generally agreed upon in the network security community that an incident response policy is a legal document that addresses how to handle a breach of security due to negligence, criminal behavior, or equipment failure. The incident response policy should be a document created jointly between the chief information officer (CIO), the general counsel, personnel, the information technology management and select employees, the company's physical security department, and the chief executive officer. It may be good to consult the International Association of Computer Investigative Specialists IACIS to see if they have existing templates of such documents that can be adapted to the organization to save time.

The incident response policy should define thresholds of security breaches and incidents as well as describe what agencies and professionals to call for to respond to each type of event. The incident response team consists of those professionals who are selected to respond to such events. They need to be trained in documentation, evidence and data collection, and the policies of the organization. They also need to be able to assess a threat that could escalate to violence and know when to advice the authorized requestor of the investigation when he or she should call physical security and law enforcement.

It is generally known that workplace violence is on the rise and a planned operation such as stealing intellectual property or defense documents from an organization poses risks to those who investigate. It is reasonable to assume that the consequences of detection and arrest are severe and the perpetrators may harm bystanders or investigators in order to flee the site with the data.

It is generally a good idea to have an advisory board for the company and discuss the risks associated with operating a business. Then one can contact a security organization such as ASIS International and discuss hiring a certified protection professional to develop a security plan and do a vulnerability assessment to learn where the weaknesses are in the corporation. Many high security facilities even look at power lines and phone lines as a vulnerability to pass data through.

House 2 – 20 Feet Away
Same Street – Same Powerlines

There was no connectivity at House 2.

(35 years old)

Home 2 was 20 feet away from Home 1.

Laptop on table

Simulation of house 2

Figure 3.6 – House 2 on the Same Street

Connectivity to Neighboring Facilities and Homes
I teach a class called Computer Security Administration. One of the students was a power line technician for a utility company while the other was a wiring inspector for a local town. The wiring inspector's opinion was that once the signal reached the transformer on the telephone, the step up and step down in voltage combined with the electrical noise of the transformer would nullify the connectivity. The power line utility technician said it was possible for the signal to continue to neighbors since there exists broadband power line service in some rural parts of the United States that use power lines as a medium for transporting data in addition to power [1].

We therefore checked the connectivity at house 2 which also had a wire that appeared to be connected to the same transformer as house 1. We also checked connectivity at a relatively new house about one hundred and fifty feet away. Connectivity could not be established at the other homes on the street. Even though connectivity was not established, it is a good idea for home users of Ethernet power line adapters using such devices in legal manners to use encryption and passwords on the power line adapters to increase security and reduce the effects of eavesdropping.

Monitoring Power Lines and Phone Lines
There are Ethernet phone line adapters as well as Ethernet power line adapters. A covert area network or unauthorized area network may carry communications between people as

well as documents on these wires in a means not addressed by policy. Could monitoring an electrical line that is carrying a conversation between perpetrators be a violation of the law for the investigator? It is evident why a lawyer specializing in electronic wiretap investigations is needed.

It is important that your computer policy, telephone usage policy, and Internet policies are well written and address a wide scope of misuse. One may wish to monitor power lines and phone lines for activity in the house or facility but listening to a phone conversion on a phone line without a warrant is a violation of the Federal Code known as Title 3 and was also discussed in the case of Olmstead versus the United States in 1928 [2]. It is therefore important that personnel have a copy of all employee signed policies including the telephone usage policy. It is also important that these policies are dated, understood by the employee and legal. The Federal Wire and Electronic Communications Interception and Interception of Oral Communications Statute, 18 U.S.C.A. 251 addresses many of these concerns.

If a manager or information technology officer is to put a power line adapter or phone line adapter on the facilities' wires to detect covert networks, it is essential to make sure this is permitted so both the manager and the company itself does not face severe criminal and civil penalties. It is therefore important that when power line networking is suspected that the general counsel, the authorized requestor, personnel, the information technology department, and the county prosecutor's computer crime task force are in communication and all responses are legal and eliminate or reduce any risk to the investigators.

Preventing the Unauthorized Area Network on Power Lines and Phone Lines

One of the best ways to stop unauthorized networks is to first have strong policies that prohibit such activities. Policies must be legal, signed, dated, witnessed, notarized, understood, and equally enforced. One mechanism to enforce such policies is to put copper sheeting in the rooms to prevent wireless transmission. Another enforcement mechanism is to use filtered power lines as described by the Tempest Standards stated in the National Industrial Security Program Operating Manual NISPOM, Department of Defense 5220.22-M, Chapter 11, Section 1, Tempest http://nsi.org/Library/Govt/Nispom.html [3].

Conclusion

In this limited pilot study, we saw that other people on the same street were not able to connect to a neighbor's network if everyone used Ethernet power line adapters. However; for the legitimate home network user, it increases security on one's network if one uses the optional encryption and password that comes with the software for the Ethernet power line adapter. It is also a good idea to turn off the broadband modem if the system is not in use.

When it comes to the insider threat, strong legal policies with a wide scope to prohibit unauthorized networks are needed. Strong policies that give broad investigative powers to the business or organization are needed so the attacker is not legally protected and the investigators are put on the defensive. Mechanisms such as power line filters and copper sheeting prevent or help to prevent emissions.

Incident response teams need to be in communication at various times with personnel, general counsel, the chief information officer, the authorized requestor, the chief executive officer, and law enforcement professionals so that up to date training in legal methods of countering, investigating, and preventing such threats is assured.

REFERENCES

1. URL Visited May 4,2005 http://www.forcvec.com/bplcoop/index.html
2. The case of "wire-tapping" Olmstead v. United States, 277 U.S. 438, 574-76, 48 S.Ct. 564, 571, L.Ed. 944 (1928) Brandeis, J. dissenting
3. Nelson, B., Phillips, A., Enfinger, F., Steuart, C., "Guide to Computer Forensics and Investigations", Thompson Course Technology, 2004, Boston Massachusetts, 2004, Page 171

Chapter 4 –
Employees and the Need for Background Checks and Policy

4.1 – The Need for Checking Potential New Employees

There is certainly a need to check to see who will be working for you because when you hire someone, you are bringing someone in to your business who will interact with your customers, handle credit cards and money, and possibly sensitive data. Educational material from Thompson Education also says that lawsuits from negligent hiring practices are on the rise [1]. Many employers will do a pre-employment screening known as a PES to see if the person's credentials, including licenses and university degrees are valid. It is easier and cheaper to background check an employee and not hire the person in the first place than to handle potential litigation from the person after an event where you decide to terminate their employment. In the UK all government employees are automatically screened through Criminal Records Branch (CRB) so that a doctor who has been struck-off, or a known pedophile or sexual predator, indeed any potential employee with a criminal or undesirable record is thoroughly vetted, with their application being rejected prior to an offer of employment.

Rick Mish, a member of the National Association of Investigative Specialists (NAIS), reports that estimates for lying about university degrees and competencies are as high as 80% [1]. When a person lies about credentials and gets hired, there are two trusts that are betrayed. The first is the employer's trust of the employee and the second is the customer who trusts the company has the competent skills to perform a job for the agreed upon cost. When I was applying for a job to the Young Men's Christian Association (YMCA), the application asked for my highest level of completed education which was a master's degree. I put down the point of contact at that University and also signed a waiver to be background checked with the FBI for criminal records. This was necessary because I would be writing reports, interacting with clients, and looking at client records.

4.1.1 – Criminal History Check / Background Check

Sometimes potential employees may willingly give the information to be background checked while others will not. You must check with your local laws where you live but most times the potential employer is allowed to take the application and contract it to a private investigator to verify the information and see if the person has a criminal record.

There are public records on the Internet that the private investigator can check. The person's name can be "googled" on the Internet at http://www.google.com. There are also a variety of databases such as Lexus Nexus and services that can be obtained through www.peoplewatcher.com. A date of birth (DOB), and Social Security Number (SSN), allow a private investigator who phones in to verify the person's motor vehicle record and criminal history check at the local courthouse. In the United States, no permission is needed to check birth certificates, civil records, voter registration lists, traffic tickets, marriage licenses, and court records [2].

Another common check is the credit check. A private investigator can use the potential employee's name, SSN, and DOB to find out all about a person's credit history: their liens, loans, and bad debts turned over to a collection agency. Data can suggest a certain individual may be a poor hiring choice; thus saving the company a lot of grief by passing that person over and hiring someone much more suitable.

A background check used in organizations could be compared to the interpersonal social practice of dating which is practiced in all Western countries. Ideally, everyone wants to get to know the person you may potentially be bringing into your family and identify those who will negatively impact on both you and your family.

4.2 – Policy and the New Hire

Once the new employee is hired, it is necessary to tell the new employee what is allowed and not allowed. These do's and don'ts, known as policies and procedures, need to be clearly explained to the new recruit from the outset. I said to a friend that some people go to work, do their personal email, check on their stocks, read CNN news, instant message some friends, and shop for gifts on e-bay. He said I just described his morning. Most likely my friend was joking but there are people who do such behavior and waste company time which causes work not to be done on time and can lead to cost overruns. There have been times where an employee has said to the employer that he or she did not know that one could not do some personal email and shopping on e-bay. Expectations of behavior need to be set in policy which puts everyone on the same page to what is allowed and not allowed [3].

Each policy needs to be created with input from the Chief Information Officer (CIO), managers, Human Resources (HR), The General Counsel (the legal advisor), and upper management. You want to have a policy that tells the employee right away what is allowed, not allowed, and any sanctions for violating such policy. This comes first in a course on network security because without policy such as non disclosure statements, you may not be able to prove something was a trade secret and the employee may not be able to be prosecute an employee who violates it.

4.2.1 – Educating the New Employee

You need to have an induction session where an employee is educated in all the policies of the company. This should be done as early as possible in the employee's career so that the policy is ingrained in the daily practices of the employee and all these policies become an automatic response to any actions because it is ingrained as part of the corporate culture [4]. The employee should receive an employee handbook and policy, an email policy, an Internet usage policy, a telephone policy, a clean desk policy, a computer usage policy, a backup policy, an information policy, and a workshop on sexual harassment that includes a test. All policies should be signed and dated by the new employee confirming their understanding and acceptance, and filed with the Human Resources Department. This will make employee infractions of security much easier to enforce and prosecute if there is a violation. Maiwald says that enforcing policy is a thankless job that requires little technical skill but sets rules and forces people to do things they do not want to do but may be the most important job an organization can do for information security [3].

4.2.1 – Policy for Discarding Paper

A company can have all the firewalls and technical security known to man but if there is no proper policy on information security, the technical security becomes worthless because low tech things like disposing of confidential material in the trash can simply compromise and undermine the best intentions. It is unfortunate that people will climb into the dumpster of a corporation and pull out trash such as paperwork or equipment. This practice is known as dumpster diving. The nursing home I volunteer at has a policy where all paperwork with public health care information that is to be discarded is shredded. The employee only needs to walk down the hall and place the paper in a locked bin with a slot. The paperwork is later crosscut shred. It is not sufficient to just cut paper into strips. A group of Iranians in 1979 were able to take bags of documents shredded into strips, spread them out in a large warehouse, and reconstruct the documents. Companies such as Church Street Technologies can offer a service to reconstruct cross cut shred documents if one accidentally destroys the wrong documents [5].

4.2.2 – The Clean Desk Policy

There exists a policy known as the clean desk policy. It exists because there are often cleaning people who are contracted to clean offices after hours. Such people are there alone with documents and computers for long periods of time and unsupervised. Cleaning people are often low paid and there are few checks done to investigate who they are hiring. There is a possibility that the cleaning people who are cleaning your office are low paid, in need of money, and have a criminal record for theft. Why put yourself and your company at risk. In the movie "Wall Street" the character played by Charlie Sheen actually becomes a silent partner in such a cleaning company just so he can obtain insider information that helps him steal a lead on the competition. It is easier to institute a clean desk policy where all papers are locked in file cabinets and all address books, notes, and other information is locked in the desk drawers. This practice of putting all papers, notes, and disks in the desk is known as "the clean desk policy." [4] It is a policy that reduces doubts about trade secrets or customer lists unknowingly being stolen after hours.

4.2.3 Information Policy

The information policy could include the regulations about the dissemination of potentially sensitive information content by paper or electronically by email, website, or through the telephone. Please look at the picture in 4.1. Please notice that the license plate is not shown nor is the location. If I wanted to show a picture of Lincoln Mercury, then the extra license plate information is not needed since it could be used for a nefarious purpose by someone; hence the picture is shown that excludes that information. That is an example of information security.

The information policy of a company could also discuss the content of potentially sensitive information sent through the mail, as well as verbal communication among clients and employees with customers and the media. The nursing home I volunteer at has an information policy with posters in the hall that remind employees and visitors not to talk about employees or residents in public places because there is a potential for a HIPAA violation. Information policy can also discuss how both public and sensitive information is stored, distributed, and destroyed. Maiwald discusses the employee responsibility to protect sensitive information [6]. The loss of some information could be a policy violation while the loss of a trade secret could be a violation of economic espionage and theft of trade secrets, Title 18 United States Code 1831 and 1832.

Sensitive information for a business might be customer lists and orders while in a college it might be grades and anything that goes to the outside world. Some offices have a policy that you must stand by the fax when receiving a sensitive information fax so others do not see it or intercept it. Some companies have an information policy regarding paper that is printed that states an employee must wait at the shared printer until a sensitive document has printed. Some people say it is often important for organizations to conduct a debriefing after a security event to explain the context in which the event happened. Some people say a witness needs to understand what they saw in the context of what went on. Many companies will have a Public Information Officer (PIO) that can speak intelligently with people outside the organization about a security event.

Figure 4.1 – Car is Displayed So as To Protect Owner's Identity

4.3 – The Need for Policy Management
As people get more and more electronic devices that can access the company's network and private networks, there is a potential for the unauthorized sharing or "leaking" of information. Policies therefore need to be updated by a policy board to reflect the dangers that new publicly available devices pose to the organization. Cell phones now carry cameras which can mean that people carrying a cell phone could take a picture of a fellow health club member in the

public shower and post it on the Internet. Cell phone cameras can also be used in a top secret facility to email documents or pictures of equipment. If the person destroys the evidence on the cell phone before it is seized, investigating the offense becomes costly and time consuming. It is therefore important to have your policy be ahead of the technology curve so you can regulate it before you have an incident. Prevention is better than cure: having a policy already in place will hopefully anticipate and help eliminate many potential areas of conflict.

A security professional I know relayed a story about a school where people were taking locker room pictures without the other persons knowledge on cell phones and uploading them to the Internet. If the subject of the picture is less than 18 years old, then this may be considered child pornography and is a violent crime. The regulations governing these are Title 18 US Codes 2251 – 2252 and the Child Pornography Prevention Act of 1996. A more responsible proactive approach to policy will stop or at least severely limit technologies being used improperly. A proactive approach can save your organization money in lawsuits, lost revenue due to bad publicity, and also harm to people by acts of crime.

4.4 – The Policy to Destroy Electronic and Paper Information

Some county law enforcement agencies hold evidence regarding a homicide for 100 years after the conviction. Some original paper documents concerning government transactions such as the Louisiana Purchase are stored for hundreds of years. However; some paper documents are defined by a policy to be of little consequence and can be destroyed after several years. There will be a policy to destroy certain memos or promotional literature after a certain date. This is known as a date of destruction and often such documents are given to a private agency that is bonded for a million dollars and guarantees the destruction of such paper documents.

When electronic documents on a computer need to be destroyed, that becomes a trickier proposition. Most people using Microsoft Windows feel they just need to right click on the document and delete it. However it is not really destroyed and only the pointer to the file is deleted. That file could still be present on the floppy disk, USB drive, or hard drive until it is written over by a new file. A better way to remove a document would be to delete as before but then use a tool such as Clean Sweep to remove the file and what is in cache memory and temporary files. One should also run the de-fragmentation tool in Windows to put all the files in order and rewrite files over blank spaces in the drive. "The erasure of sensitive electronically recorded information from obsolete and excess digital archives can remove the risk of embarrassment or other problematic events if such information is taken out of context. Private communications between various parties including contractors may also pose security risks [7]."

4.5 Policy to Protect the Organization's Information Assets

Information on the computer is at risk when an employee leaves the organization. That is why there is a termination policy. The employee may leave and go to a competing company so there is both a non-compete agreement, and a non disclosure agreement. Information on any network can be at risk if and when new operating system software updates, new application programs, or new hardware is introduced to the system. That is why there is a change control board policy. We also need to protect the information from system failure or lightning, so there is a backup policy. We also need to discuss the email policy, computer usage policy, Internet usage policy and telephone usage policy.

4.5.1 – Termination Policy

The termination policy is necessary because when an employee separates from the company, he or she may want to cause the company harm if the circumstances were unpleasant. The person leaving may place a logic bomb in the system that wipes out all information after a certain date or when a trigger mechanism is activated. The person leaving may try to take digital information or property that belongs to the organization at the time of separation. That is why many companies will have a security guard visit the person leaving approximately 30 minutes before termination and accompany the person off the premises. Upon leaving, the termination policy may state that the access control badge to the facility must be surrendered to the security guard along with any photo identification badges. Documentation may even be required to be signed by the person leaving confirming and recording that all employment termination procedures have been duly met.

It might also be a good idea to disable the person's account thirty minutes before their employment is terminated so they do not send any nasty-grams or download loads of company assets to take with them to use at their new job. If a person whose employment was terminated and states they forgot personal property, an escorted visit might be the proper policy to insure nothing harmful was placed in the workplace and nothing of value was stolen. If there is no criminal activity that is investigated within the following year then the disabled account may be deleted if no regulations prevent it. However; it is a good idea to save the account because saved files or communications may be useful if a criminal investigation occurs. The System Security Certified Practitioner (SSCP) book has some great information on termination policies.

4.5.2 – Non-Compete Agreement

The non-compete agreement must be fair and realistic for it to be enforceable and hold up in court. The non-compete agreement is a legal document that limits the employability of an employee who could take information to a competitor. The non compete agreement might state for example that an employee making a certain network component cannot work at a local competitor's company that also makes the same network component for a period of six months. The non-compete agreement is important so that trade secrets are not lost to a competitor. Such information on non-compete agreements and non-disclosure agreements is important for the network security certification called the System Security Certified Practitioner (SSCP) which is the precursor to the CISSP certification which is discussed in a future chapter.

4.5.3 – Non-Disclosure Agreement

The non-disclosure agreement means that one will not reveal proprietary information to any party not specified in the agreement. It is a way to protect intellectual property which is an asset of the company. Though proprietary information is not considered capital by most people, it is an asset that can be sold or used to generate products and wealth. It is important to make sure that any employee who is leaving has signed the proper non-disclosure agreements and does not have access to such information before the termination of service occurs.

4.5.4 – Change Control Board Policy

Employees of a company may hear about a great program or piece of hardware that will enhance security, increase productivity, facilitate communication, or simplify daily work. There has to be a protocol to introduce new equipment, processes, and configurations to hardware, software, and all network connectivity regarding wires, fiber, or wireless. There needs to be a policy that all employees are aware of to introduce change to equipment, software, and connectivity within the organization. All change should be recommended to a change control board that can review the new change, analyze it for potential vulnerabilities or harm, and then sign off on it. Once it is signed off, it can be introduced to an information technology manager who can reconfigure the company's hard drive image to include that program or system file change, and then distribute it to each computer on the network.

Most companies and university computer labs have adopted a common standard of equipment, software, and connectivity for all the machines in that facility. This standardization means that a problem machine can quickly be isolated and have a part swapped out and the hard drive can easily be re-imaged with a standard image of the organization and it is back to normal, just the same as all the others. This kind of uniformity allows for a high level of support not possible on a network where each machine is different and many specialists are needed at all times. Standardization means that large inventories of various parts need not be kept. Each machine is mapped on the network and a support person can easily send the hard drive image through the network if enough bandwidth exists and the software can be restored.

The change control board often consists of people with policy and technical backgrounds. Each board member will read the Carnegie CERT website to see what programs should be updated, what operating system patches have been tested and stop vulnerabilities yet make few side effects, and what chipsets need to be updated on modems and computers. Change control board members should also read trade magazines, attend local technical conferences when possible, and network with other information technology managers to constantly keep updated and to see what security issues they are dealing with. More about change management can be obtained in the System Security Certified Practitioner (SSCP) study guide on pages 135-139.

4.5.5 – Backup Policy

The backup policy needs to be developed by the upper management and the Chief Information Officer and then handed to the information technology managers to implement. Employees need to be educated on the importance of backing up and how lost data can ruin a company or leave it vulnerable in a lawsuit. Many companies have now outsourced backups by having all employees saving everything on their directory in a network drive. Then the outsourced security company connects to the company who wishes their data backed up and backups each person's individual network drive as well as all company data. This transfers responsibility to the company who is contracted to back up the data. Some companies that keep the backups insure the data and even claim their underground facility can survive a limited nuclear attack.

Many companies that have employees do their own backups will have the employees do a full backup of everything once a week and have a policy that incremental backups or that day's changes are backed daily. The policy may state that a designated trusted person do the full backups once a week and deliver them to an offsite location that is climate controlled and tamper proof on a weekly basis. The same person may also be the one designated to pick up the backups if an event takes place.

4.5.6 – Email Policy

The email policy should state if attachments are allowed or not. Viruses can be hidden or embedded in .exe files that are received by the company. People who often send each other funny jokes or movies may, unwittingly, actually be spreading malicious code embedded in the movie or .exe file. The anti-virus policy may also state that all email must be scanned for viruses both coming in and going out. The email policy also needs to state if personal email is allowed and how much is allowed if it is.

Email should also discuss content of what is allowed to be discussed and what is off limits. Ethnic jokes could cause a lawsuit. Many jokes are offensive too and could lead to public embarrassment of the company and fines if they escaped to the public. The SSCP test preparation book states that a person may send a joke if it is put in a special encryption known as "Rotate 13" or "ROT-13." [10] This is where each letter is shifted 13 places. An 'a' becomes an 'n' and a 'b' becomes an 'o.' It is the same principle used in the Caesar Cipher of ancient times where letters were shifted by three. The plaintext of 'cat' would be the ciphertext 'fdw' in Caesar Cipher. The person deciphering is risking being offended. The email policy may also be to use a web based interface much like Hotmail because allowing email on a system is one of the biggest security risks a company can make because of malware that is embedded in attachments.

4.5.7 – Computer Usage Policy

When it comes to computer usage, I once worked at a community college where a supervisor caught a worker and sitting playing FreeCell as in Figure 4.2. The employee said he was getting familiar with hand eye coordination and getting accustomed to the personal computer as his supervisor requested. This was in the year 1993 when people were getting used to graphical user interfaces known as GUIs and moving from operating computers with DOS command line prompts to GUIs. The supervisor mumbled some words and said to stop playing games and do some real work. Computers were new to most employees at that time and a computer usage policy had to be quickly developed.

I teach an ethics class and an introduction to network security class. At the beginning of the semester I decided I would pose a simulated problem to both classes of students. I surmised the network security class would see the need for a computer usage policy and the ethics class could discuss some of the ethical considerations. Suppose Smalltown Memorial Hospital receives a donation of a dozen computers, network equipment, and even installs them in the hospital. In our simulated problem, the hospital administrator took a look at the computers on the network and saw no games and just regular applications. He gave his okay for the employees to use the computers to support their work. The night shift of nursing comes in and the employee takes her break at 3 AM and the weather is bad and cannot go outside. She goes to the computer and types in FreeCell at the DOS prompt. The game starts and she plays it.

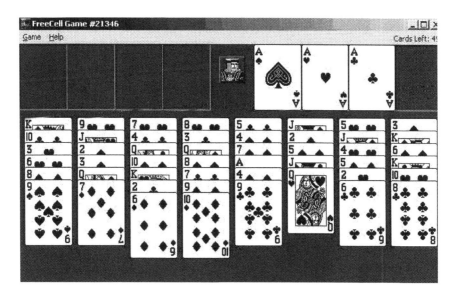

Figure 4.2 – FreeCell, On Most Microsoft Windows Operating Systems

My classes had students of all levels of management and entry level employees. Some were in healthcare while others were not. One person said that if she was the nursing supervisor, she would allow games on the night shift for people on break because often one cannot leave the floor if there is inadequate coverage such as when employees are off work with the flu. The same person said she would rather see a nurse playing games and able to hear a patient in distress rather than sleeping if things got slow. Another person said the nurses in a hospital are busy during the first two shifts and would never think of playing a game at work! Another person said what a person does on their break is their own business as long as it does not break any laws or policy. Another person said a break place should be separate from the workplace to differentiate things. It was a topic that evoked strong feelings and debate on the first day.

One student who once did some Public Information Officer (PIO) work for an organization asked how would that hospital look in the news if a nurse was rightfully playing a game on break and a patient died during that time? The students said the risk of such a negative event and its impact on the hospital is greater that a person's right to recreate on break. After that I purchased a book called IT Ethics Handbook and each possible dilemma such as the one with games has a liberal and conservative viewpoint expressed for each ethical question. [9]. I found Stephen Northcutt's book excellent and answered a lot of questions I was cautious to voice.

This whole discussion of games on the network shows you how a seemingly small issue can lead to heated debate and possible bad press and have a negative impact on the organization. It should help you to understand how important a computer usage policy is, and how having such a policy can pre-empt difficult decisions.

4.5.8 – Internet Usage Policy

The employee needs to know how much time he or she may use on the Internet at work and in what context. Is personal email allowed and under what circumstances and for how long? The policy needs to specify the purpose, scope, and responsibility. The policy needs to be enforced uniformly in the organization and be thoroughly understood by the employee; with a documented recorded that is individually signed, dated, and filed in human resources. This document must be on hand in case there is an incident that the incident response team investigates. The signed policy will show the employee knew what he or she did wrong and will give the organization the ability to impose sanctions.

Without a signed Internet usage policy, it will be difficult to discipline the employee who was surfing the Internet, shopping on e-bay, or who simply says everyone else does it. The policies cannot just be enforced on the employee who may be loud, obnoxious, and considered the "problem child" everyone wants to see fired. Policies are to be understood, signed, dated, filed, and enforced equally among all employees.

Stephen Northcutt's IT Ethics Handbook also mentions how we need to guard against the employee who misuses instant messaging and browses objectionable material at work. In the United States, pornographic screen savers can make a hostile workplace and lead to serious consequences for the offender.

4.5.9 – Telephone Policy and Network Security

You may wonder why I mention a telephone policy in a book about network security. Suppose an employee brings in his or her computer at lunch time and uses the laptop's modem to connect to his Internet Service Provider and to chat on an Internet singles website. The male employee's actions could relate to something of a sexual nature. Suppose the man or woman at the other end of the conversation may also be an on duty off duty employee. Then the communication could be considered sexual harassment depending on some circumstances. It is commonly known that sexual harassment can occur between the same sex as well as the opposite sex. The event could bring bad publicity, fines, and negatively impact the image of the organizations which may drive customers to a competitor. Since a telephone can be connected to an acoustic coupled modem or the RJ11 connector can also be disconnected from the phone and placed in a modem, then it becomes necessary to have a telephone policy.

Most people would think a telephone policy only governs long distance charges for non business related calls as well as using up company time talking to people about none work related conversations. Therefore, we all need to start to think about how computer equipment can be partnered with connectivity at work; whether it is phone line, wireless, fiber, or through electrical wiring in the building. Then a policy needs to be developed that regulates telephone usage or wireless technology use before you have an event that is costly and may lead to litigation.

REFERENCES

1. Mish, R., (1996),"Background Investigations", Thomason Education Direct, Study Unit 0580070, Private Investigation Course, Pages 1-2

2. " ", Page 9

3. Maiwald, E., (2001),"Network Security, A Beginner's Guide", Osborne – McGraw Hill Publishing, Berkeley, California, ISBN 0-07-213324, Page 55-58

4. Jacobs, J., Clemmer, L., Dalton, M., Posluns, J., (2003)," SSCP, Systems Security Practitioner Study Guide, Syngress Publishing, ISBN 1-931836-80-9, Page 148-9

5. Url visited May 2005, http://www.churchstreet-technology.com/SHRED_FAQ.htm

6. Maiwald, E., (2001),"Network Security, A Beginner's Guide", Osborne – McGraw Hill Publishing, Berkeley, California, ISBN 0-07-213324, Page 59

7. Url visited May 19,2005 http://www.planitroi.com/pana_address_data_security.cfm

8. Jacobs, J., Clemmer, L., Dalton, M., Posluns, J., (2003)," SSCP, Systems Security Practitioner Study Guide, Syngress Publishing, ISBN 1-931836-80-9, Page 146-7

9. Northcutt, S., (2004),"IT Ethics Handbook, Right and Wrong for IT Professionals", Syngress Publishing, Rockland, MA, pages 38-39

10. Jacobs, J., Clemmer, L., Dalton, M., Posluns, J., (2003)," SSCP, Systems Security Practitioner Study Guide, Syngress Publishing, ISBN 1-931836-80-9, Page 327

Chapter 5 –
Access Control and Auditing

5.0 – Introduction to Chapter 5

This book is taking you through a logical progression starting with chapter one where we first looked at a location to keep our computer and network connection. We examined the structure, the electricity, and risks such as flooding. Then we discussed self insuring. In chapter two we looked at creating a network with connecting various personal computer platforms with a common workgroup using a building's existing electrical wiring. We also examined dial up accounts, and connecting to private networks as well as the Internet. In chapter three we examined how people can use a network for nefarious purposes such as spying. In chapter four we examined the need to background check potential employees, and outlined a series of policies to set boundaries on acceptable behavior and sanctions for non-compliance. In chapter five we will assume we have hired our new employees and wish to control access to what systems and applications they can use. We will also look at auditing in this chapter to make sure we keep systems working properly and how they can be properly monitored.

5.1 Introduction to Access Control

The need to control computer or network access will exists as long as there is the possibility that an unauthorized person may access a local or remote account or an authorized person could access an area of the account with computer files that he or she is not allowed to access. Access control can be low tech and physical, such as in a lock on a door with only one person who has the key. Access control can also be high tech and use devices that compare some aspect of what makes us unique to an established pattern such as a thumbprint. The practice of using a unique aspect of a human for identification including access control is known as biometrics. The most common access method you are probably familiar with is the username and password. However; the problem is that any password can be forgotten and writing it down simply compromises the security. A password can also be guessed by another person making it less secure. Once you think about the username and password and compare it to the biometrics, then you should see that the biometrics is a much more secure method of authenticating a person so that access may be granted.

5.2 – Biometrics

Biometrics is a new more reliable way of insuring definitively that the person logging on to a system is in fact the person who they actually say they are. Some people have expressed some concern about using biometric devices because they feel that their fingerprints or iris image is stored in the machine and a hacker will then be able to access the stored image, or even more basically that the whole process impinges on their civil liberties. Their worry is that the hacker will create a mold from that image and use that fingerprint in a crime so the owner of the print gets blamed. It is my opinion that such fears are unfounded. The manual for the thumb print reader made by Biologn says that the information about the print is stored in a vector that uses between 10 and 70 points minutiae points and even if a person knows where such data is kept, it will be difficult to use it for unauthorized purposes [1]. I have spoken to information security specialists that tell me that the information about the biometric data including retinas and prints are coded in very long vectors and are in proprietary formats that most hackers would not have access to.

5.21 – Thumb Print Reader – Decentralized Access Device

Thumb print and foot prints were used in ancient China. They served as a means of identifying and authenticating famous or wealthy people. The thumb print might be used on a clay seal. It could be used for a comparison to identify that specific person much like finger print cards in the early 20th century in the USA. The lines we see on the thumb are generally known today as friction ridges. The business community in ancient Iraq also used thumb prints in clay for the same purposes as those in China. Could the ideas of using thumbs prints a means of identification for important transactions have traveled along the silk route? In the year 1856 Sir William Herschel, a magistrate in India, began to use handprints on documents. He did this because often imposters or other rogues would confuse the issue or even maliciously refute a transaction. It is very difficult to deny you entered into a business transaction when your handprint is on it.

An example of a finger print can be seen in figure 5.1. The Biologon 2.0 thumb print reader I used on my Windows 98 machine will use information about my thumbprint and store it in a vector. The location of a dot could be described in Cartesian Coordinates on the x-y plane. Such information can go into the database for the application. Perhaps the location of a whorl might be stored. The whorl is a round labyrinth like shape. The bifurcation is where one ridge branches out into two ridges. The delta looks like a fine piece of crystal used to hold champagne at a party. Any raised line is known as a ridge. The end of a ridge is known as an end. There is a system known as the Henry System that was invented around the beginning of the twentieth century that someone could study to learn more about fingerprints and their classification.[3] Television shows such as CSI have increased interest in fingerprints.

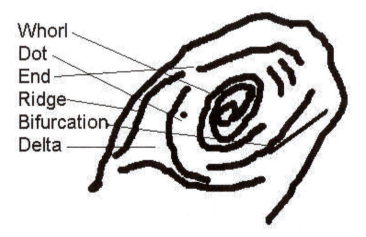

Figure 5.1 – An Artists Rendition of a Fingerprint

A thumbprint reader can be installed between the keyboard and the desktop computer. The bootup process will not be completed if the thumb print is not given and verified. Some thumbprint readers also require a certain temperature because people also have varying temperatures.The thumb print biometric device is on a remote desktop and the login process does not use a centralized computer. Therefore the thumb biometric device for desktop computers is a decentralized device.

5.22 – Hand Geometry Biometric Device – Centralized

The hand geometry device is often coupled with other input and biometric devices as a means of multi-factor authentication. The hand geometry device, for example, might be connected to a main computer at the nursing home which authenticates each person and logs them in an auditing system to keep track of the entry and exit times of all employees and volunteers. Multi-factor authentication means that more than one set of means will be used to authenticate who you are. Many times we must show a drivers license and a social security card as a means of identifying ourselves and proving we are United States citizens when applying for a job. I will give an example of how such a hand biometric device was used to identify employees and volunteers at a local nursing home.

Each person who was a volunteer at a certain nursing home had to show up at a certain day and be interviewed and fill out a form. Then each volunteer also had to put their hand on a device that looked like a steel plate with what looked like 5 golf tees on it. The golf tees went between each finger and around the outside of the hand. The shape of each person's hand is unique. Each volunteer had to do this procedure three times to insure an accurate measurement was made and any variation in measurements could be noted.

The device also had a numeric keypad on it. I was given an 8 digit number to memorize and I was to type it in a dozen times. I typed the number in about the same speed each time. The number was an identifier as was the speed at which I typed it in. Then each time I go to the nursing home, I type in my number at a certain speed and put my hand in the hand-geometry device. I am authenticated and logged in. When I leave, I do the same process and I am authenticated and logged out.

5.23 – Iris Recognition

The iris of each human is unique and also acts as a good biometric. Some iris recognition systems are expensive because they must use a high quality camera system. Therefore some manufacturers will combine an iris recognition system with a video conference system so as to make the investment more worthwhile. I have been told informally that in New Jersey there exist some county prisons, "correctional facilities", using iris recognition for logging people in and out of the system as well as identifying the inmate population and others.

5.3 – Access Control Methods

Jacobs and Clemmer state that the United States Department of Defense recommends the Orange Book for standalone computers. The book uses four grades with various levels to classify the level of trust they can put in that operating system's security. [4]. The Orange

Book shows Grade A having a level A1 which is "verified protection" and this is the highest level of trust in the model. The operating system Boeing SNS and Honeywell SCOMP have this rating. The next grade down is B and consists of B1, B2, B3. The systems trusted IRIX and ACF2 fall in this mandatory access control level. Grade C is the next grade down and consists of C1 and C2. It is discretionary access control. Jacobs and Clemmer show in their chart that Novel Netware and Windows NT fall in here. Grade D has no level and means minimal security. PalmOS and MS-DOS are grade D. Jacobs and Clemmer also say there is also a Red Book that is for computer networks. [4]

5.3.1 – Discretionary Access Control

This is a system you may be familiar with if you have used the UNIX operating system. It allows the owner or system administrator to set permissions on who can read, modify, and execute a file. It is level C1 or C2. There is an Access Control List (ACL) that assigns each file an Access Control Permission (ACP). Jacobs and Clemmer say Windows NT and Windows 2000 use this system too. In my opinion it is quite popular and is worth learning because of its widespread use and since it is part of the body of knowledge needed for the System Security Certified Practitioner (SSCP) certification.

5.3.2 – Mandatory Access Control

Jacobs and Clemmer say Mandatory Access Control (MAC) can be found at many military institutions. Perhaps your company may win a bid and will obtain a defense contract. Some of the employees who may work on the project may work in various compartments of the project or will use the computer network to work collaboratively. In any case they will need to get a security clearance. A security clearance is a process of checking a person's past to use an indicator of trust. A person getting checked for a security clearance will have their credit history examined for bad debt such as a home beyond far their income or perhaps excessive debts from large purchases or gambling. Large gambling debts could be an indicator that one could be compromised in order to pay off those debts. A person's driving record is also checked. A driving record with various offenses listed may indicate disregard of the law or carelessness. Both traits are not desirable for working on projects and networks where national security could be in jeopardized. The criminal history must also be checked. The mandatory access system employed by the military uses a system of clearances such as top secret, secret, and classified.

Perhaps you may feel the background investigators are too nosy. My opinion as a computer science doctorate holder, and not that of a licensed private investigator, is that these kinds of safeguards are absolutely essential. It is just my opinion so please do not take it as fact. Let us use a short story to illustrate a point. Robert Kreitner and Angelo Kinicki have a text called, "Organizational Behavior." It is used at Fairleigh Dickinson University in management classes. Many students indicated they liked the text because it talked about employees of various personality types and work habits. The text also described these employees in some work situations, and then described possible outcome scenarios after certain events happened. It was my opinion after reading this text that employees with certain habits and personality traits, in certain situations, can often be predicted to act in certain ways. We are all individuals with a free will but our behavior is probably more predictable then we care to admit. Perhaps the background check is a way to identify various types of employees and match them to security levels commensurate with the level of risk they pose.

Suppose Lucretia is a great scientist but often spends her time at the gambling hall or at the track and spends far more than her salary. She has some big debts. A defense contracting company is considering hiring her and trusting her with proprietary secrets worth hundreds of thousands of dollars. Bobby, the lab director, has a background check done on her during the initial hiring phase. Bobby's competitor companies are also known to drink at the same bar as Lucretia. Do you think Lucretia is a good risk for hiring and giving a secret clearance to?

5.3.2.1 – Top Secret
Jacobs and Clemmer say the top secret classification is the highest in an organization. In World War 2, the English had a place called Bletchley Park where they did top secret work of breaking German codes. The Germans did not have a clue their codes were being broken partly because of the English code breaker's respect for the top secret clearance. The leak of the top secret fact that the English could read many transmissions would have been devastating to the war in the North Atlantic. Top secret matters affects national security and sometimes the national security of other countries and the leak of top secret information is devastating to that country.

5.3.2.2 – The Secret Clearance
In the world of clearances, the designation of secret is of a magnitude lower than top secret. If there were documents that were labeled secret, and they were leaked to a competing organization or unfriendly government, it would be less devastating than if the documents were top secret. However; it would be very bad for that company or government who owned the documents. They might lose reputation or lose a competitive edge they once enjoyed.

Suppose a person is working at a civil engineering company on a project such as a new sewer treatment plant for Iraq. The person needs to follow certain protocols like the clean desk policy. All the plans, disks, CDs, and maps would be locked in a safe or file cabinet before leaving the office to go home or to lunch. The person who is being cleared for secret clearance would probably have their neighbors interviewed by a security organization. The nature of the investigation would have their credit history, criminal record, and driving record examined and reported on. The investigators would also interview various coworkers and perhaps clients too.

5.3.2.3 – Public Documents
Public documents are often put on a website. They may be distributed at a trade show or in promotional literature concerning the organization. Public documents are often included in part or their entirety in annual reports, 5 year plans, or as a link on the company website. It can be placed in the company prospectus and will have no adverse consequence at all if read by anyone once in the public domain.

5.3.2.4 – Confidential

Anytime you see a designation of confidential, you know it is real personal data that could reveal work habits, health problems, absenteeism, personal grievances, or certifications held, or grades earned. It could also be about financial transactions between the company and the employee. The leak of confidential data could embarrass employees or even be a violation of HIPAA but it would not be devastating to the company unless it was forced to pay a fine for wrongful disclosure of personal data.

5.3.2.5 – Unclassified

The unclassified data is hard to categorize and cannot be packaged into the classifications we discussed. The disclosure of unclassified information would not have much impact on the company. Some security professionals say data that was secret many years back may often be "declassified" and given a designation of unclassified.

5.3.2.6 – For Internal Use Only

This is a classification for any document that is only for inside the organization. Internal use means it stays completely within that organization. You don't even fax it to a supplier, a contractor, or even share it with an affiliate. It is private internal correspondence or facts and could cause hard feelings or public embarrassment.

5.3.2.7 – Need to Know

We have all seen movies where someone said the data can only be accessed on a *need to know basis*. This usually means if someone has a top secret clearance, that person may only access items that are pertinent to that investigation or project they are assigned to. Suppose I had a top secret clearance and went to the archives of the United States Air Force. I can't for example look up everything associated with the B1 bomber or the A-10 Warthog for my own curiosity simply because there was a story about it on the military channel on television. An investigator needs to only look up the facts that are relevant to the case he or she is working on.

5.4 – Checking the System Logs – Auditing

There is a formal process for auditing that we will discuss later in the book. I am going to loosely use the word "audit" here for the purpose of examining transaction file results in depth. It is important that someone reviews or audits the security logs for the system to investigate if a storage or input device is failing often and not allowing users to do their tasks in a timely fashion. In Windows XP, try going to Control Panel, Administrative Tools, Event Viewer, and then choose one of the logs to view (see figure 5.2). My CD-ROM often fails and wastes a lot of time as the system log reveals.

Security logs are also important because the person whose job it is to check security can also see whether or not there are a lot of attempts to access a system that someone is not authorized to use. Every time a drive is accessed or something happens on the system, there is a transaction created that logs either a success or a failure. You can imagine the number of entries in the log! Depending on your system, it is best if you discuss with a software vendor if there is a tool that you can purchase for your operating system to help automate viewing the system logs for suspicious activity.

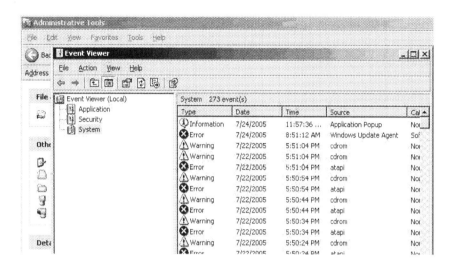

Figure 5.2 – The Event Viewer and System Log

5.5 – Photo ID Cards

It is a really good idea for an organization to have photo identification badges for all volunteers and employees. I am a volunteer at a local nursing home that recently adopted a system of photo identification badges. My name is printed across a bright purple color in a rectangle that identifies me as a volunteer. My picture is updated every two years, so it remains current. My signature is on the back of the photo ID Card that I wear on a lanyard around my neck so that if a security guard may think I am not the person on the picture, he or she can stop me, check my picture, and ask me to sign a piece of paper and compare the signature on the badge. In the post 9-11 world, security should be the rule, not the exception. A natural progression from ID Cards is the Smartcard. Credit card size Smartcards with built-in microprocessors can store huge amounts of digital information, and can be configured to be multi-functional (e.g. open doors in restricted areas; automatically raise car-park barriers; double up as lone-worker emergency alarms, etc) as well as serve as ID Cards.

I went to a Homeland Security Conference at a military base one time to learn more about information security. Each person who attended was given a lanyard and an identification badge. It took approximately 30-40 seconds from the time I stood on an X on the floor until I was wearing the badge. The process was amazing. I walked into the building, took a conference materials folder, and stood in line. I was then instructed to stand on the X while a picture was snapped with a digital camera. I handed the man my business card which was scanned in a small machine about the size of a breadbox. He put a white plastic card about the size of credit card in the machine. Then out came a photo identification of me that my information bar coded in the ID and a small photo of me appeared in a hologram of the conference on the ID. It would be extremely costly and time consuming for someone to forge such an identification badge. I felt it was a good idea too because people at the base could see who I was, what I was there for, and point me to what exhibits I should be looking at.

I was at an American Society Industrial Security (ASIS) International meeting and was telling everyone about the impressive portable photo identification card system that I saw. I was wondering how I would find out about it for a Homeland Security Conference at Fairleigh Dickinson University. Then I found out that an ASIS International member named Bernard Younghans, sells such a system for All Star Identification Systems Incorporated. His email is byounghans@visitorwatch.com.

All Star Identification Systems Incorporated (ASISI) has an access control system that is outstanding for colleges and universities. The system allows a visitor to a college dorm to get a picture identification badge after handing in a strong credential such as a driver's license. The driver's license can be scanned and kept on record along with information about the person's visit. If there is a fire or a security event that happens, both police and fire safety officials know who is in the building. This helps simplify the rescue process because a list of the visitors and residents can be generated and compared to those who were evacuated from the building. Fireman would not need to risk their lives looking for possible victims who were trapped in the building. If the fire was not accidental, such a list would help an arson investigation by providing potential witnesses or suspects.

5.6 – Hardening the System with Passwords
One can make the operating system more secure from unauthorized access by requiring the system to use password complexity: this requires using upper and lower case letters and numbers. The password can also be required to be changed once a month: by setting the expiration date. You can also require that the password be 11 characters long so even if they had a computer dedicated to cracking your password, the password expiration date would be up first before the dedicated computer could crack the password.

In Microsoft Windows XP for example, you can go into Control Panel, Administrative Tools, Local Security Policy, Security Settings, Account Policies (see figure 5.3). Then go into account lockout policy. Here you can change a threshold setting so that after three tries the user is locked and out and may not try again until the duration setting allows for another change. People will often set up the system to allow three tries and then lock the person out until another 30 minutes later. There are a variety of simple low cost things you can do with your system before you need to go out and purchase a thumb print biometric device. You should also disable the guest account.

5.7 – Access Control Systems
Access control systems are an important part of the security process but no element of security by itself is the answer. There needs to be a security policy or plan which addresses system security, physical security, network intrusion, employee screening, and constantly assessing vulnerabilities and addressing them. The access control systems play an important part of allowing computer networks and visitor control centers in buildings to monitor, audit, and regulate both human and system traffic.

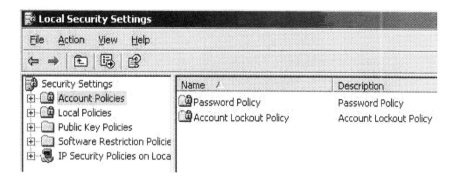

Figure 5.3 – Password Settings for Microsoft Windows XP

REFERENCES

1. Biologin 2.0 Users Guide, Part Number 010-BL2-ENG-002, 1999 Indicator Tech. Inc.
2. URL Visited April 5,2005 http://onin.com/fp/fphistory.html
3. Simms, J, Butt, L., (1996), Thompson Education Direct, Private Investigator's Course, Fingerprinting Techniques
4. Jacobs, J., Clemmer, L., Dalton, M., Posluns, J., (2003)," SSCP, Systems Security Practitioner Study Guide, Syngress Publishing, ISBN 1-931836-80-9, Page 61-62

Chapter 6 –
Great Applications to use on the Network - Telerobotics

6.0 – Introduction to Network Applications

In Chapters One to Five we've spoken about creating a network, connecting to the Internet, and even controlling access. However; what are you going to do with this network? Some of the great network programs that exist are: MS Outlook for email, Netmeeting for video conferencing, and a program called e-team that allows first responders a means of communicating and tracking an event in real time. Let's look at Netmeeting in this chapter and see how useful it can be by itself and as an object in programming.

6.1 – Video Conferencing Netmeeting

Before starting Netmeeting, it's a good idea to make sure the sound and video equipment you are using works properly. First make sure the speakers and a microphone are both hooked up properly and all connectors are in tightly. It is a good idea to pretest the microphone and speakers by using Microsoft Sound Recorder which is found in accessories. Sound Recorder is an operating system utility used to record voice your and play it back. It is also a good idea to ensure that whoever you video conference with has basically the same type of operating system and peripheries (i.e. webcam, etc) so that both your equipment configurations are as compatible as possible.

It is also easy to test the webcam to make sure it is compatible with Netmeeting. Just click on Netmeeting and click on the picture of an eye to see if the webcam works. If you previously heard yourself with "Sound Recorder" and can now see yourself with the webcam in Netmeeting, you are ready to video conference.

The application called Netmeeting is a great program that comes bundled with Windows 2000/ME, 98, and early versions of Windows XP Home Edition. You have to put the arrow on the bottom right of your display and get the IP address. (This can be found by looking up Programs, Accessories, Command Line, then typing the following DOS command, IPCONFIG /ALL. Then you email your IP address to the person you are going to video conference with. That person can also email you their IP address. One of you can then start Netmeeting and place a call by clicking on the icon of the telephone and placing the other person's IP address in there. A Netmeeting session between Gary Stephenson in England and Dr. Eamon Doherty at Fairleigh Dickinson University in Teaneck is taking place below (see figure 6.1).

Figure 6.1 – Netmeeting

The person called will get a message asking if they will accept the call. Once "accept call" is clicked, the two parties are connected and can see and hear each other. The system was half duplex. This means that one person would talk and then the other could listen while the other talked. Two-way simultaneous, full duplex sound was not possible. The Netmeeting application allowed one to adjust the window size of the person who who's talking. There is a volume control to adjust the sound. There is a chat feature that allows two people to type to each other in case the sound is lost. One of the best features for collaborative work is the whiteboard. I found I could be discussing how to design and operate a telerobotic system and then use the whiteboard to draw a picture, cut and paste artwork, and speak at the same time. The person at the other end could draw on their version of Netmeeting's whiteboard too, showing simultaneously the same content.

6.2 – Using the Remote Desktop Feature in Netmeeting for a Telerobotic Arm
Coauthor Gary Stephenson built an OWI-007 robotic arm and interface kit in England. The robotic arm cost about Seventy Five United States Dollars (USD) and contained 250 pieces. The interface kit contained 50 pieces which Gary had to solder. Gary learned to solder from a movie I created and mailed over on a CD. I also gave soldering tips while video conferencing with him using Netmeeting.

Netmeeting is a standalone program available with many versions of Microsoft Windows but it is also an object that can be added to programs that you can create using Microsoft Visual Studio or Visual Studio .NET. The Netmeeting object just has to be dropped and dragged in the visual C++ or Visual Basic program you create and then you will have the ability to use a webcam, share computer desktops with others, and video conference. Adding Netmeeting to my robotic arm interface took it from being a program to control a robotic arm in my office to be a telerobotic system controllable from anywhere in the world with an Internet connection. We only needed to start the program, connect with the Netmeeting object, allow remote desktop sharing, and we could control each other's robotic arms across continents. If Gary had a programming problem, I could start his version of Visual Studio and correct Visual Basic .NET source code if he needed me to.

I found it was best if I used the T1 connection at work which gave me 100 Megabits per second to video conference on. The computer I used for teaching at work was a dedicated computer that only had the robotic arm application and MS Windows Millennium operating system on it. If someone was able to hack in, there would be nothing of any value on that machine since it was only for the robotic arm and videoconferencing. I would invite my students in and we would work on a paper collaboratively with Gary Stephenson in England.

The best part was when we could allow remote desktop sharing at our end in New Jersey and Gary would start a robotic arm program and operate the robotic arm in my office, from his study in Tynemouth, England, (over 3000 miles away). He could see in my office and operate the robotic arm to pick up objects. He would use the interface and talk to us and tell us how to improve the robotic arm program. It was a fabulous session because he would talk to us and test our robotic arm on my desk in real-time during the practical lesson.

Bruce Davis, a quadriplegic man who tested many of our applications, could also use a brain computer interface or electromyographic switch to operate the same robotic arm with the same program. Our idea was to allow Bruce Davis (see figure 6.2) to be able to work remotely at any factory in the world, even China. The motivation of the telerobotic arm was to make it possible for people to work between any two locations, regardless of disability. It is an application of the recurring concept of international collaboration that Thomas Friedman speaks of in his book, "The World is Flat." [1]

Bruce Davis operated the robotic arm by viewing a menu that scanned robotic arm functions. The cursor would visit a button that said "arm up" and stay there for two seconds. If Bruce wanted to make the arm raise, he would make a face while the cursor was on that button. The transducer converted that impulse into a left click. There were 15 buttons, so it took 30 seconds to visit all the buttons. It was a slow system if you missed a button, you had to wait 30 seconds for the cursor to visit all the buttons before it came back. It is much like missing a bus and waiting a period of time for the next one. Bruce was able to do quite a bit of work with the system. Bruce has also successfully operated the same robotic arm on Channel 50 New Jersey News television in New Jersey. Upon viewing a video of this session Gary Stephenson later wrote a robotic arm interface, using Visual Studio, which considerably speeded up the throughput time for choosing button options, making it much more intuitive to use, and less taxing on the user.

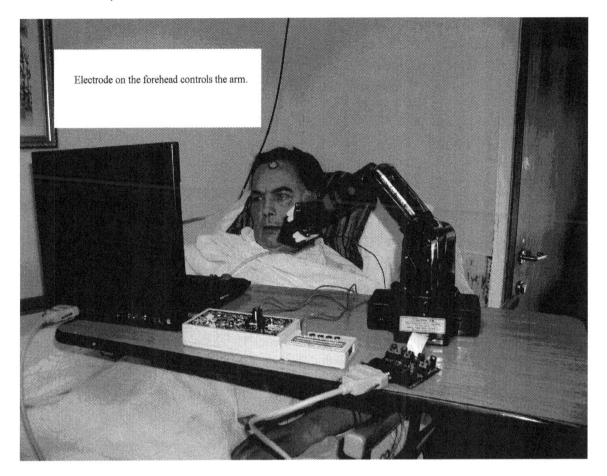

Electrode on the forehead controls the arm.

Figure 6.2 – Bruce Davis Operating the Robotic Arm with a Facial Electrode

A robotic arm that has five moving joints is said to have five degrees of freedom. If a robotic arm has three moving joints, is said to have three degrees of freedom. Bruce Davis operated a robotic arm with five degrees of freedom. The interface he operated controlled a two pincers, a wrist, and elbow, a shoulder, and a base. The program worked in such a way that a Netmeeting object was embedded in the robotic arm interface and a call had to be manually made to the remote location with the robotic arm. Then when the connection was established, control could be given to the disabled person. The disabled person could then work independently for hours. The disabled person had complete control of the desktop computer at the remote location with the robotic arm. The only security aspect we were concerned about was raised by another author of a network security book, Chey Cobb, who said that a Netmeeting leaves all 64,511 ports open which leaves your firewall wide open. We thought this posed a major point of vulnerability, especially from hackers looking to find and access your machine by port scanning everyone connected to your ISP [2].

6.2.5 – Early Attempts to Use A Robotic Arm

The United States Army often uses the model of crawl, walk, and run for developing and deploying systems. I will now compare my system of development to this one for any military scientists who are readers. I was in the crawling stage when I connected a Cyberlink Brain

Body Interface to Bruce Davis and used what was known as a C.A.T, Computer Aided Tracker, to move the cursor on a computer screen with buttons to control a robotic arm. Bruce used the Cyberlink and C.A.T. with an interface that I developed in Visual Basic 6.0. My interface used a variety of rectangles that I defined and sent to an Application Programming Interface (API) call named ClipCursor. The rectangles connected to form paths (see figure 6.3). The cursor could only travel on those paths. Bruce used thoughts and face movements to move the cursor around the screen to touch buttons that activated the arm. It was slow and required precise facial movements and intense concentration.

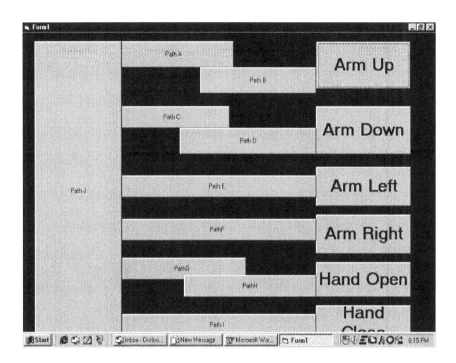

Figure 6.3 – Visual Basic 6.0 Interface for Robotic Arm

The walking stage was when we used the Don Johnston sensor switch or the Cyberlink for only making a left click. We had the program automatically visit each button every two seconds. Examples of robotic arm movements on buttons are: arm left, arm right, hand open, hand close, arm up, and arm down and then it would cycle back. In the walking stage, we used a Radio Shack Armatron robotic arm with three degrees of freedom. If you wanted hand open, you just waited until the cursor landed on that button and clicked by using the electrode on your face. We were in the running stage when we used the OWI-007 robotic arm with five degrees of freedom, added a Netmeeting object and a webcam, and made the robotic arm program telerobotic and usable between any two points in the world with internet connections.

6.3 – Telemanipulator Versus Telerobotic Arm

There is a lot of specialized vocabulary concerning robotics and sometimes the definitions are difficult to understand for people with a non technical background. That is why some people have asked me the difference between a telemanipulator and a telerobotic arm. The telemanipulator is a mechanical system used for handling objects in close visual proximity.

One usually stands behind a giant glass enclosure about 4 feet from the object being moved. The objects that are manipulated with the telemanipulator are usually contaminated with radioactivity, skin irritant, or by some type of biohazard that you wish to stay away from. The telemanipulator is worked by turning two prosthetic arms and handles that allow you to move the object in question but stay at safe distance behind glass. The Atomic Testing museum in Las Vegas Nevada has a telemanipulator that the public can use to pick up and examine a contaminated core sample that originated deep in the earth.

The telerobotic arm is a robotic arm that can be operated from large distances, even across continents. The telerobotic arm can be controlled by a person from one country using a computer, who watches webcams and listens to microphones to get real time feedback about what they are both doing. Sophisticated telerobotic arms and computer aided telemanipulator systems have even allowed a doctor to perform tele-surgery between Italy and The USA.

6.4 – Motivation for Robotic Arm and Telerobotic Arm
The robotic arm system was created by Dr. Eamon P. Doherty and students for a paralyzed person to be able to do work at home. When a network was used, network applications such as Netmeeting were embedded in the robotic arm interface to incorporate webcams and remote connectivity. At that point we had a telerobotic arm. The motivation of the telerobotic arm was to allow a quadriplegic man to work anywhere in the world and not be limited by distance or disability. We hope to see a world where people, regardless of disability, can operate machines from various parts of the world and collaborate on projects to help mankind in a positive way despite the condition of local economies.

REFERENCES

1. Friedman, T.,(2005),"The World is Flat, A Brief History of the Twentieth Century", ISBN 0-374-29288-4
2. Cobb, C., "Network Security for Dummies", Wiley Publishing, Page 247

Chapter 7 –
The Layers of The Network and Limiting Connectivity

7.0 – Introduction to the Network Layers

This book has talked about creating a network and using specialized applications such as the telerobotic arm on it to facilitate work. However; we have not defined the layers of the network and examined the components of the network itself. We will look at the seven layer OSI model here. We will also examine limiting connectivity and some of the various types of security your facility may be interested in.

7.1 – Emissions Security

Perhaps you work at a company that does research and development (R&D). R&D is very expensive and time consuming. When a company puts resources into R&D, it often takes years to develop a product, market it, and recoup the initial investment, let alone make a profit. R&D may also not lead to something profitable. It is reasonable to assume that there is much to be gained by stealing the R&D of a competitor. Eaves dropping on a competitor, also known as industrial espionage, could be done by employing a hacker to intercept communications between a company and its parent company or on selected computers. Emissions security could be considered the protection of electronic signals emanating from electronic equipment, including cordless telephones and computers.

It is generally known that old cordless telephones in the United States work on frequencies of around 49 megahertz. It is possible that a person in close proximity to your home could intercept such conversations with a scanner. A scanner is a radio that sweeps a preset set of frequencies and selects a frequency with activity. This is why it would be a poor idea to have old cordless telephones at work because a person could sit with a scanner on public property or a street nearby and eavesdrop. You could employee emission security at your office by replacing the old cordless telephone with 900 Megahertz phones that use spread spectrum technology. Spread spectrum technology was invented in World War Two by the Hollywood actress Hedy LaMarr and composer George Antheil for the purpose of sending control signals to torpedoes. It allowed a transmitter and receiver in synchronization to send data across frequencies in a random pattern [1].

There are also stories on the Internet about people in vans disguised as utility company vehicles who park the vehicle on a public street outside of companies doing R&D. These vans use a directional antenna to collect signals going over cables to a printer. The van would have a printer inside and be able to print what was going to the printer inside the company. Directional antennas are also capable of picking up signals from keyboards at distances of one half mile. The United States Government created and deployed a special type of computer equipment known as Tempest that reduces emissions considerably and significantly increases communication security [2]. One can also find stories on the Internet about Tempest and Black Hawk Canyon where many communication security devices were tested.

7.2 – The TCP/IP Model and Security

There are various ways of explaining the layers of a network. There is a TCP/IP model with four layers described. Those layers are the application layer where applications such as telnet are used to connect to remote computers. Another popular application is ftp, File Transfer Protocol. Ftp is very useful for many home computer users because it can be used to transfer files from a home computer to a website. It can also be a security risk because a hacker could connect to your machine and remove files. Ftp should not be enabled if you are not going to use it. It is generally a good idea to get someone to help you go into the control panel in whatever version of Windows you are using and turn off services that you will not need. I no longer use ftp and telnet so I turned them off. Another application most network users depend on heavily is SMTP, Simple Mail Transfer Protocol. It allows people to use email. Domain Name Server (DNS), allows something like a set of four pairs of numbers to be mapped to a domain name such as www.eamondoherty.us which is much easier for us humans to remember.

There is also the "Transport Layer" underneath the application layer. If the protocol TCP or Transmission Control Protocol is used, then there is a connection to the destination and a steady stream of bits are packetized and numbered. These packets then move to the Internet Layer. The packets are numbered in the transport layer and flow is controlled only if the TCP protocol is used. The User Datagram Protocol (UDP) has very little error recovery and is connectionless and used for broadcasting [3]. There is also a TCP/IP stack where bits are placed on for further transportation.

The "Internet Layer" sends everything to various networks. Packets get routed by a router all around the Internet until they get to the correct address. An IP number consists of four pairs of numbers such as 232.45.54.2 and there is a way of looking at those numbers and determining the country. Packets may arrive at their destination out of order because of error and resending or rerouting in some cases, but since they are numbered, they can be reassembled in order. A bit like a train who's carriages all leave the sending station in precise order (e.g. 1,2,3...etc) and eventually arrive in exactly the same order at the receiving station, regardless of the separate lines they may have happened along in the meanwhile to get there.) The "Host to Network Layer" is the lowest layer that would include signals and wiring. Tannenbaum says there is little literature on this level.

7.3 – The OSI Model of Network

The acronym OSI stands for the Open Systems Interconnection and this model was developed by the ISO, International Standards Organization. You might have heard of ISO 9000 which is a standard that people everywhere aspire to abide by. Level one is the physical layer that is concerned with signaling, wires, and fiber. Sometimes you will hear network security professionals refer to someone as a "layer one man". That means he will be really interested and have expertise in cable transmission speeds and know how long each type of cable can be run in an office. Such a designation means you are hardware orientated and care about the bits and bytes. Margolis says the physical layer, "Manages putting data onto the network media and taking data off" [5]. The coaxial cable, fiber optic cable, hub and switches, twisted pairs, untwisted pairs and wireless Ethernet radio waves, router/switches, and repeaters are all members of the domain of level one [6].

The second level from the bottom of the OSI model is the Data Link Layer. Margolis says, "the data link layer is responsible for passing data from one node to another" [5]. Each computer on the network has a MAC, Media Access Control, address. Now it is possible to change the MAC address in the Windows operating system but every network card and every network device in the world has its own unique MAC address. The router can use the ARP, Address Resolution Protocol, which locates any device on the network so it can receive packets of data. Some people can even change the ARP cache switch so traffic can be diverted from the legitimate destination to an alternate one. Encryption can be used to deter such activities [7].

Next time you are connected to the Internet, just **go to the DOS prompt on your computer and type in ipconfig/all and it is not case sensitive. You will see an IP address as well as physical address such as 48-3F-34-55-1B-22. This consists of are six pairs of hexadecimal numbers making 48 bits. Hexadeci**mal is a base 16 numbering system used by many computer professionals as a sort of shorthand for binary. There are many excellent books on data processing math that teach you how to convert binary into hex. Let us quickly look at an example 0010 = 2. We see nothing in the 8's placeholder, nothing in the four placeholder, but see a 1 in the two's placeholder. Now lets count in hexadecimal and we start with 0,1,2,3,4,5, 6,7,8,9,A,B,C,D,E,F, to10,11,12,13,14,15,16,17,18,19,1A, etc… Let's look at A=1010. There is a 1 in the 8's placeholder and nothing in the 4's placeholder, and 1 in the two's placeholder. We then have 8+2=10 in decimal or A in hexadecimal.

Let us now consider layer three, the Network Layer. This acts like the Internet Layer in the TCP/IP model. Try going to the DOS prompt next time you are connected to the Internet. Then type in TRACERT www.fdu.edu and it is not case sensitive. You will see the routing to the Fairleigh Dickinson Website. You may see a dozen hops that it takes to there. Each hop will have an IP address and a listing of a physical location. It looks much like a bus trip with a stop in several towns. Think of that if you send me an email and each one of those systems has a copy of the email [8]. System administrators can look at, and effectively monitor what kind of traffic passes on their system for security purposes.

When you send an email to me, it will take many paths to get to me as we just learned. Many routers along the way will look at the address and check their Access Control Lists (ACL) and may pass it on to somewhere else, reject it, or send it to a person on the network whose MAC address is listed in the table of that router. The Internet uses an arcane mechanism known as the "Border Gateway Protocol" (BGP) that is used by hundreds of Internet networks to advertise routes to direct traffic. There is a fear that hackers can use this to disrupt the Internet [10]. This is a real problem because many of our systems, such as e-team that let disparate groups work together and use the Internet as a tool to communicate and operate a Common Operational Picture (COP) of the event, can be so easily compromised, and the consequences would be catastrophic during a terrorist event or natural disaster, both of which seem to be happening with more regularity nowadays.

Layer four is the transport layer and it takes care of connection-oriented packets used in TCP which has some error recovery capability and sequences packets. This layer is so important because it limits the flow of bits and bytes. (**N.B**. A bit is an acronym for *b*inary dig*it*; and there are eight bits in a byte).This layer fastens the top three layers to the bottom four. The transport layer also takes care of User Datagram Protocol (UDP) packets as we discussed in the TCP/IP model earlier. People use UDP in streaming video. It is not important if I lose a second or two of video if watching "Casablanca" with Humphrey Bogart on my system. Many hackers will use a port scan on this layer to see what ports you have open on your IP address on your machine. You can ask someone to help you turn off ports with Windows XP full edition. People use port 21 for ftp and port 23 for telnet, and port 25 for SMTP for email [9].

Layer five is the layer that is known as the "Session Layer." This layer creates and terminates a connection and establishes a common method that the two machines will use such as half duplex in Netmeeting for sound. Half duplex, simplex, and full duplex are the methods that can be employed for determining how data will be sent. Full duplex is data that flows in both directions.

Layer Six is the presentation layer which handles encryption as well as compression schemes. Miller and Gregory, others of a network security preparation manual, also point out something I have not seen in other books discussing the OSI model. They say that layer six can convert characters from EBCDIC to ASCII [11]. This means that certain data from IBM mainframes can communicate with PCs on the same network if configured properly. Miller and Gregory also discuss that layer six uses common format such as GIF, Jpeg, or MPEG to represent image sound and video formats [11].

The application layer is layer seven, the highest layer, and uses File Transfer Protocol (FTP), Hyper Text Transfer Protocol (HTTP) for websites, and a variety of other services that probably are crucial to most computer users.

7.4 – Creating a Storage Area Network

There are times when you want to have a computer network in your home to share common documents upstairs and downstairs. However; you don't want everyone going in your machine to get the document and you don't want to go in other family member's computers. Suppose you are writing a book like I am and sometimes work upstairs, downstairs, or in the kitchen. I may be working on Chapter Three in different places depending on what books are nearby. Soon I ask myself where is the latest version of Chapter Three? Did I write that great bit about computer warfare upstairs or downstairs or in the kitchen? Where is it? I need to have a Storage Area Network, commonly referred to as a SAN.

The SAN uses a Redundant Array of Independent Disks (RAID). My storage device on the SAN only accepts transactions from three machines. It knows the machines by their 48 bit MAC addresses. I once pulled the Ethernet plug on the SAN and pulled out the power without shutting down and six months later I stared it up without even a document lost. All my computers in my residence connect to the storage device and all documents are saved there. The hard drives on the machine are only for the Microsoft Office, Windows, and some programming language software. The idea of the SAN is for there to be one common place to get and store documents so there is no confusion upon versions. I recently added an uninterruptible power supply to the SAN and the computer I use most often because the power is often disrupted 5 minutes or more daily due to storms or over demand by air conditioners. A security professional told me that it would be in my best interest to show you a conceptual picture of the network and not show a picture with brand and model information. Figure 7.1 shows the conceptual drawing of a SAN.

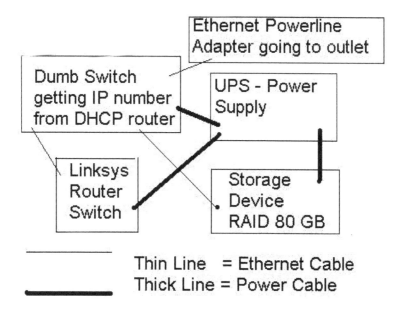

Figure 7.1 – Storage Area Network

Each old computer gets an Ethernet card or Belkin USB-to-Ethernet connector and then plugs into an Ethernet power line adapter which is plugged in the outlet also known as an electrical socket. There is a wizard available in Microsoft Windows to help connect you to the network. The storage device might be drive E to everyone. Each computer in the house uses the electrical wiring in the house to connect to the storage device in the basement. Since each computer never connects to the Internet, I don't care whether it has Windows 95, 98, or any other operating system. I don't need a firewall or updates because it is only internal. The funny thing is that if another family member or guest is working on a manuscript with me, they can use Netmeeting to video conference with me since the Linksys router switch provides a local IP number for each machine and the storage device. The video conference aspect means they don't have to leave their chair and can keep working until they need more coffee or need to stretch and walk around.

There are also books on how to create your own Storage Area Network. Many people use them to centralize their important data folders: photos of the family, tax records, their kid's homework, work taken home from the office, and also to archive materials. The SAN is a great configuration and the RAID technology is advocated by great minds such as Richard Grigonis, author of Fault Resilient PCs [12]. However; it is still a good idea to take one of the newer computers with a CD burner, and burn a CD or two of important folders with important files. Then put the CDs in one of those CD albums. This is a way of backing up your system. Backups are important because nearly every piece of computer equipment I known has failed terribly at least once since I owned it.

7.5 – Organization of Files and Information Security

I know this sounds very basic but if you can't find a document that you need, it does not matter if some hacker deleted it or you lost it, it is unavailable to you. One of the basic security tips I tell my students is that they can give files names that are meaningful to them. I have a file called 2003tax.xls and it is kept in a folder called home2003. I create about 10 gigabytes of documents and photograph's a year as a professor, author, scientist, regular member of society. In order to be able to retrieve such materials, I need a good naming schema for my folders and file names. It is also a good idea not to include sensitive data on files that could be accessed by others. You can go to the chapter on access control again and review some principles there if you wish. My tax file includes my expenses and charitable donations and income but does not have my social security number. I also do not put my date of birth in the computer. That is practicing some common sense information security.

7.6 – The CIA Triad

The CIA Triad is not something Langley, Virginia; or from the movie, "Men in Black" It is an acronym for Confidentiality, Integrity, and Availability (CIA).

Confidentiality means that sensitive data is only viewed by those who should see it. Confidentiality is regulated by access control. If you realize you have neither the technical skills or ability to make your system secure, then don't connect to the Internet and keep your all your data on a thumb drive that you lock in a file cabinet after each use.

Availability is the other issue I addressed before. The file needs to be available when I need it. I don't care if the file is lost because a hacker deleted it or because I have gigabytes of files with meaningless names in unorganized folders. The file needs to be available when I need it. If the security is too strong and I cannot remember the password with upper and lower case letters, the result is the same and I cannot access the document when I need it. Natural disasters such as flooding or lightning storms can destroy data on paper or in electronic format. It is necessary to have a backup of the data in a safe place offsite and it is important to protect the building where your computer is from flooding and lightning as discussed in chapter one. It might be a simple lightning rod is all you need. In any case these natural disasters can cause you to lose data and make it unavailable.

REFERENCES

1. Grigonis, R., (2000),"Computer Telephony Encyclopedia", CMP Publishing, N.Y., N.Y., ISBN 1-57820-045-8, page 481
2. Maiwald, E., (2001),"Network Security, A Beginner's Guide", Osborne – McGraw Hill Publishing, Berkeley, California, ISBN 0-07-213324, Page 7
3. Margolis, P.,(1999),"Computer and Internet Dictionary",Random House Publishing, ISBN 0-375-70351-9, page 577
4. Tannenbaum, A., Computer Networks, Page 38, Third Edition, ISBN 0-13-349945-6
5. Margolis " ", Page 403
6. Jacobs, J., Clemmer, L., Dalton, M., Posluns, J., (2003)," SSCP, Systems Security Practitioner Study Guide, Syngress Publishing, ISBN 1-931836-80-9, Page 397
7. Jacobs " ", Page 402
8. Chesbro, M., (2000),"The Complete Guide to E-Security", Citidal Press, ISBN 0-8065-2279
9. Jacobs, " ",Page 403-405
10. Bank, D., Richmond, R., "Information Security, Where the Dangers Are", July 18,2005, The Wall Street Journal, Page R1
11. Miller, L., Gregory, P., (2003), "Security+ Certification For Dummies", Wiley Publishing, N.Y., N.Y., Page 31-33
12. Grigonis, R., (1996), "Fault Resilient PCs", Flatiron Publishing, N.Y., N.Y., ISBN 0-936648-89-9

Chapter 8 –
Vulnerability Assessment

8.1 – Introduction to the Vulnerability Assessment

Suppose someone who has a home computer wants to get an idea of how vulnerable their computer is to unauthorized access and misuse. The person could hire a professional who is certified as a white hat hacker. They could also have some friends play the role of various members in a vulnerability assessment team and examine each aspect that contributes to vulnerability and then address each of those points.

Sometimes you might go to someone's home and be surprised to see a computer on in the living room with a broadband cable modem near the family's cable TV. It is probably there because they have a signal splitter. It is convenient to set it up there and connect to the broadband cable connection though it is not the best location from a security point of view. You may be surprised that there are no special accounts on the computer's operating system and no firewalls installed. Everything is accessible to everyone. This is probably because they are "not tech" people and thought computing was a good thing and never examined any risks. The situation is worsened when these people have teenage kids with unsupervised access to the computer while the parents are at work.

I have been told before by a couple male students that the above situation describes their situation well and they would joke about me talking to their wife to learn of their situation. Such students will often be the ones calling home at the class break time and telling their family to please turn off the computer until they can secure it. They may be greatly distressed until they rectify the situation.

8.2 – Physical Security

The computer and network is accessible to any of their children's friends who come over. The kids may go to some music website and can download music from websites which often have loads of spyware. If the minors access pornography, this is illegal and will often result in malware getting downloaded on the home computer. Now we will look at some countermeasures to limit physical access and theft.

The computer can be put in a room with a lock and key. The windows should have working latches and the room should not be accessible from the attic. The kid's friends could also walk out with the desktop computer in the above situation. A locking cable or proximity detector might be in order. One piece goes in the desktop, while the other piece goes in a drawer. If the desktop goes off the property, there is a 110 decibel screech until it is within the proximity of the other unit. Most people will drop equipment that sounds such a loud alarm. Many people feel cables, lock, proximity detectors, and secure rooms are measures that are too Draconian. Perhaps you are right, we were just exploring some possibilities. You have to find what is correct for your style and budget.

8.3 – Access Control for Physical Access

A few years ago I taught a very diverse student body of graduate students and some gifted graduating seniors a class called "Introduction to Network Security". The diversity was a plus because there were a lot of different viewpoints and the class was highly interactive and very animated. I looked forward to teaching the class because of the great questions and the student's desire to learn something very useful to protect their digital assets as well as prevent identity theft. Many of the students realized their computers were vulnerable and could not wait to start on my assignment of a security plan to access vulnerabilities and secure their machines. One student even told me about getting billed for books he did not order from an online book company. He also said he never got the books so he just paid the bill. Many students in the class who heard that had similar stories and then just wanted to restrict access to their computer. One student said she lives alone and came home to find all kinds of computer windows opened on her machine and the cursor was in a different place that she thought it was before. This was a sign of intrusion.

I asked the students to first look at limiting physical security. Since many had roommates who would use their personal machines without asking, some students immediately moved the computer to a bedroom that they could lock. If the machine was held in common, then they would seek a solution to limit access. One student found a product called AxCrypt that he purchased and installed. He liked it because the machine would boot up partially and then ask him for a password. He got three tries to put in the correct password. If he failed, he said the drive was permanently encrypted until it was sent to the company who sold the product.

When the computer boots up, one gets the opportunity to push a key such as F2 and access the BIOS. You can then add a password to the BIOS and save it. The next time the computer booted up, it asked for a password. The system would not fully bootup without the password.

One of the students in the class who people referred to as "the rich kid" said he bought a keyboard for his desktop computer that included a swipe card and a thumb reader biometric device. It is important to state that access control devices have fallen drastically in price in the last few years. The student with the special keyboard said he used multifactor authentication for his access control. He had to first type in a bios password, put in his thumbprint, and swipe a smart card that he kept in his wallet. Then he also had an account for his Windows system administrator account that he had to give the password to. Another student brought in a special USB drive with a lock program. He told me his machine would not fully boot up until he put the USB drive in the desktop computer. One man in the class showed us a special wireless device that unlocked his computer while he was within four feet of it and locked the operating system if he ventured more than four feet away. These were all good access control methods.

I told the students that I used a password protected screen saver that went on after 4 minutes of inactivity. This would prevent a lunch time attack. That is when people wait until you go to lunch and then they access your machine. When it came to physical security, I asked everyone if someone can walk in and unplug your cable modem and computer equipment? You need to formulate a series of questions about who is supposed to be near your computer and if intruders can easily walk in, access it, steal it, remove the power, or break it.

I once had a job years ago where I did many computer repairs and was surprised that computers on the first floor were sometimes damaged by bathroom flooding. Sometimes some people with behavioral issues in the building would flush a roll of toilet paper and keep flushing. This was a form of vandalism and you should also position your computers in your home or office to avoid problems from potential leaks. I was told a "safe path" to collect the computer and take it out. The people moved soon after.

8.3.5 – User Accounts
I then asked people if the computer is held in common. I also asked if anybody can access your accounts? Many just had private email accounts and that was that. Then the person whose machine it was, created a system administrator account and gave people accounts and directories. It is not difficult to do in Microsoft Windows. In Microsoft Windows XP they went into Control Panel, User Accounts, and made an account for each person and turned off the guest account as in figure 8.1

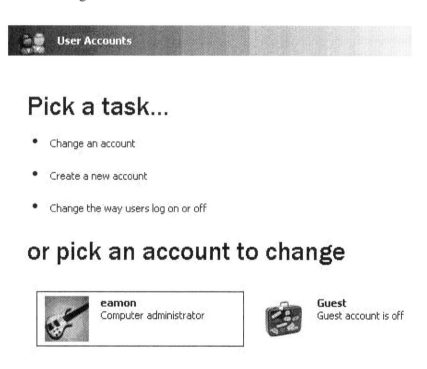

Figure 8.1 – User Accounts

8.4 – Unauthorized People Who are Connected Wirelessly
Many students from my class said they lived in densely populated urban areas and in wooden structures. Many used wireless networks but were not sure if others were connected to their network or vice versa. A person who is connected to your wireless network for example could potentially commit a cybercrime such as luring a minor in a chat room and the investigators would see your IP address and visit you. If the alleged crime is of sexual nature such as luring,

such news travels fast and one's reputation may always be questioned by some neighbors even if there was no guilt established. Therefore it is best to control access and reduce the risk of unauthorized access to your system. You can go to your DOS prompt nd type in NETSTAT –A and hit enter. You will find that all machines that are connected and listening on various ports will be listed.

I asked the students how would they know if someone could connect with a wireless card in their laptop at the end of their driveway or in the street. People were confounded and thinking of some fancy equipment they needed to purchase. A police detective said, "How about walking to the end of your property and in the street and see how far you can connect to your wireless router / switch. People were amazed at the simplicity and effectiveness of his answer. Some security is just low tech common sense. There are even websites you can go to and get the download speeds. Please see chapter three for details on getting download rates.

Some people with wireless IP cameras put them on the router in the house so they can check on the nanny. These are known as "nanny cams." There was a show on television that showed some men in a sport utility vehicle driving around a neighborhood with a wireless connection and a laptop and picking up the wireless camera video as they drove slowly around the neighborhood. This is commonly known as a "war driving attack" [1]. Perhaps this is how some of these intimate movies of Hollywood types get out there on the Internet.One can also go to electronic appliances retailers and purchase a wireless network connectivity tester for $25. You just need to push a button and you get a beep and light emitting diode lights if a wireless network of a usable strength is detected.

8.5 – What about Your Discarded Papers and Equipment?

You would be surprised that some phone answering machines, copy machines, fax machines, and printers have non volatile memory that hold hundreds of images of papers that you were faxed, or printed, or copied. When you put them out at the curb, anyone can legally pick them up and take them home. If the person is unscrupulous, they may examine the memory and see what "goodies" are in memory. This is a quick road to identity theft and in fact they may not only have the information but an exact copy of a deed, driver's license, airline tickets, or passport you copied or faxed for a vacation. When one throws out a computer, it is not enough to have deleted the documents and reformatted the machine. That just means the pointers for the files are gone but the information is still there in the drive until it is written over. It is also terrible when a person has an active dialup account for an Internet Service provider on a machine and puts it at the curb. Many of these accounts have a username and saved password. What do you do with your paper? I know someone who says they crosscut shred all their personal papers and junk mail and then put it in their fireplace. This seems like overkill but it shows the other end of security when people take it to an extreme. Crosscut shredding in my opinion is good enough unless it is something that concerns national security.

8.6 – Ever Use a Public Computer to Access Email?

I was surprised to find out that many public computers at the conferences have spyware on them and send all email addresses, usernames, and passwords to people. Sometimes people will have a "keycatcher" on the back between the keyboard cable and female connector on the desktop. The little keycatcher is the size of a cigarette butt and can be removed after a few hours use. Everything that was typed in that day is held in its memory. It can hold up to 32 kilobytes. One starts up wordpad, types in a password or hits a key combination, and a dump of everything typed in occurs. Sometimes people who you think are bird watching or harbor watching are actually using binoculars to collect usernames and passwords. Even if they cannot see the letter or number, the location of your finger tells them the key.

There are four countermeasures you can use to thwart such data collectors. You can first pull your jacket open and create a cape to cover what you type. Some people call this a "privacy hood." This will stop people shoulder surfing behind you or watching from a distance with binoculars. Secondly, you can check the keyboard jack in the back for a keycatcher. Thirdly, you can use a portable security appliance from Red Cannon Security called the Fireball Keypoint [2]. This device is plugged in the USB port of the drive on the machine you are using and works as a token with a suite of tools to keep your information confidential. The device does a spyware scan and gives one a stealth browser to secretly check websites without leaving a trace. The Email can be done on its secure client and all the temporary files, cookies, and traces of evidence are on the USB security appliance instead of the machine. It is also 128 MB and allows ample safe portability of documents and files.

Suppose you are operating on a low budget and do a vulnerability assessment and realize you must use public computers at a conference. There are low cost procedures you can implement to remove temporary information such as username and password from the cache memory. In Internet Explorer, please go to Tools, Internet Options, Content, and then on to Auto Complete as in Figure 8.2 on the next page. There is an option to clear passwords and clear forms. I feel these should be done automatically by the operating system. I do not know why form clearing must be done manually but it must be done that way. Perhaps it is for convenience. In any case one has to think of all the vulnerabilities. If vulnerability exists, one should consider doing a counter measure. This is the thinking behind a vulnerability assessment.

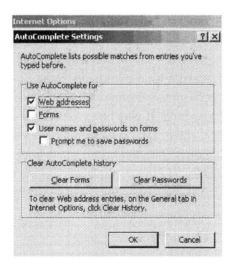

Figure 8.2 – Clearing Passwords and Forms

8.7 – Leak Test

One of the concerns you should have is that while you are connected to the Internet and even using a firewall to stop unauthorized traffic, data is covertly traveling through a port that is reserved for a trusted application. This means that even though I am using a firewall and closed ports and stopped services I do not need, data could be leaking through the firewall to the outside world connected to the Internet. That is why you need to run a leak test as a part of your vulnerability assessment. The leak test is available from places such as Atelier and such programs are easy to run. They basically tell you that while connected to the Internet, perhaps one of your trusted programs was leaking data. Then you need to reconfigure the firewall and try again until the leaks stop.

8.8 – Penetration Test

There are a variety of things you need to do in a vulnerability assessment to determine where the weaknesses in your system are [3]. One of the things you can do is determine the strength of your firewall. We saw that the leak test tested the firewall from the inside going out. Now we wish to test the firewall from the outside, namely the Internet, going into the system. There are websites such as the Symantec Website that allow you to run a penetration test to see if a packet of data can punch through your firewall. The leak test and penetration test are important parts of assessing the firewall as you can see because it is very easy to have a false confidence in such products. However; because such tests are breaching the security of a system, it is necessary to get the permission of your Internet Service Provider (ISP) and your employer, if applicable, because such tests could be a violation on policies that impact your employment or status with your ISP [4].

8.8.5 – Testing Your Backups

Most people have never tested their backups and often find out their backups were not done properly until it is too late. It is important to try restoring a backup sometime to see if it works. There are many reasons why a backup can go wrong. One might be that the backup tape drive does not work or that the media is stored in a ridiculously hot place where data is destroyed. I once left a disk with student information on it about in my old Chevy. I had also left a keyboard with in the back window. I parked on a hill in an open field going to the Sussex Airshow in New Jersey. They had various military and historic planes and it was a nice quiet family event. The windows were all the way up and I closed the vents. I was about a half mile from my car and I heard a loud explosion. When I came back, a State Policeman and people were near my car and I noticed most the glass in the back window was no longer there. I asked everyone what happened. It was not a car bomb. When the car cannot ventilate properly and gets extremely hot, the hot air will sometimes escape with great force through even an imperfection in the window. The keyboard must have got so hot that it was twisted and the disk was not even readable. My mechanic also told me that overfilled spare tires have also exploded in the car trunks at his gas station during hot weather.

8.9 – Social Engineering and Employees

It is also important that you educate your employees not to give out usernames, passwords, and other important information to strangers in person or on the telephone. Such "con games" are called "social engineering" and used to gain access to the system. Such unauthorized access could lead to identity fraud, embezzlement, or a multitude of other criminal activity. Many employees want to be helpful and have the best intentions but unfortunately that is what some of the bad guys are counting on.

8.9.5 – Are Your Policies, Signed, Filed, Enforced, Legal, and Up to Date?

I cannot stress enough how important it is to have up to date policies signed by everyone in the organization and filed with human resources and the IT department. It is also important that the employee agreement, non disclosure agreements, telephone policy, Internet usage policy, computer usage policy, and backup policy are understood, enforced equally, and legal. It is also important to have warning banners displayed on computers are bootup time to remind them of right to privacy issues or that there is none.

8.9.9 – Conclusion

There are many questions and vulnerabilities that you need to look for. I did not go through all of them. I did not look at contractors or cleaning people coming to house to do work when you are not there. You need to sit down and explore all the possibilities of how you are vulnerable and ask yourself what you need to protect and what you have to spend on protection. In an extreme case where you work from home on defense contracts, you may need to establish a perimeter and alarm system around your home office. Please also remember that poor legal documents and inadequate education and enforcement leave your company open to litigation if something bad happens. That is why there is a risk management department at your company and your insurance company who insures your home office.

REFERENCES

1. Miller, L., Gregory, P., (2003), "Security+ Certification For Dummies", Wiley Publishing, N.Y., N.Y., Page 137
2. "Tech Talk", Security Management, March 2005, ASIS International, Alexandria, Virginia, Page 38
3. Miller " ",Page 295-296
4. Northcutt, S., (2004), "IT Ethics Handbook", Syngress Book, Rockland, MA, ISBN 1-931-836-14-0, chapters 2,3

Chapter 9 –
Watching Your Family's Activities on the Internet

9.0 – Introduction

Perhaps you have seen the British comedy show called "Keeping Up Appearances." One of the things that people find comical is that Onslow and his wife are stuck with their in-laws: her bizarre father in law and his sister in law. It is never explicitly discussed but one perceives Onslow is the "guardian" or "power of attorney" for the father in law. The members of the extended family get into all kinds of trouble because both characters are "not all there" so to speak. However, a 'real life' situation similar to this fictitious one would not be funny if you were stuck with relatives in need of supervision and they stayed home and wanted to get into all kinds of trouble on the Internet with your computer. While reading this chapter, perhaps you may wish to quietly identify family members who might be at risk or susceptible to various addictions concerning the computer and network, and then discuss strategies to keep them safe with both licensed psychologists and computer security professionals.

9.1 – Addiction to Video Games

It is generally known in academic communities who follow counseling that there is a whole body of literature that discusses addiction to standalone and network video games. Dr. Chiu, Lee, and Dr. Huang have an excellent article that discusses video game addiction in children and teenagers in Taiwan [1]. One of the places you can check for video game addiction is with your child's teacher. Research indicates that video game addiction in children and teenagers in Taiwan, is associated with levels of animosity, social skills, and academic achievement [1]. Chiu, Lee, and Huang, suggest there needs to be a partnership between the child, the educators, and the family to keep video game playing in perspective so that it does not impair the child's ability to do well in school and to also develop and form meaningful social relationships and interactions. I am not a psychologist and cannot offer a professional opinion but that also sounds like good advice for American and U.K. teenagers, teachers, and parents.

An extreme case of addiction to networked games for adults was reported by the Milwaukee Sentinel staff writer Stanley Miller [2]. Video game addiction is not just for kids. And it's not an isolated phenomenon – in the UK bored adults who have the financial resources are becoming more and more addicted to games and on-line gambling, by virtue of the fact they have instant gratification. There are even widows groups for wives and girlfriends of video game addicts. Stanley Miller's article reported about a young man who put the hour's equivalent to holding a full time job into playing a game with other people on the network. The game takes place on a network and has groups of people operating virtual characters who banded together on an adventure to get treasure for example. The time frame appears to be medieval. They often play together nicely and occasionally double cross each other. Sometimes people will even sell special charms or weapons for real money on online auction houses that will enhance their performance in the game [3]. When you give up going to work, spend real money on items to enhance your gaming, and limit your social relationships, you might want to seek professional help because it appears the gaming is out of perspective in its importance to your life.

9.1.1 – Internet Gambling

One of the dangers that exist concerning Internet gambling is that since it appears to be a video game, it might not seem real. Therefore if it appears to be less real, people may get caught up in it and not really fully sense the impact of what they are doing. Some pop up windows for online casinos show gaming environments that appear to be a late 1990s video game with primitive graphics and sound. However; if you gamble online, you will need to give them your credit card to debit and credit depending on your betting and outcomes. Internet gambling may or may not be legitimate because we really do not know where the online casino is located. The casino could be a front to get your credit card number or perhaps it is in a country where it is not regulated properly if at all. Some people who are in poor financial shape may not have the willpower to stop which could cause them to reverse a small fortune to a large debt.

Some Internet gamblers will try more outlandish strategies to reduce their losses on the Internet. They may first select an Internet video game suite that has games that they are interested in learning and practicing on. Some games give advice and tell you what you did wrong. One can practice on a casino game such that is very lifelike and fun to play. However; some of the casino games you get in the mail also ask for an Internet account and give you the opportunity to go from being a video game to an interface to a real casino. The player may have a false sense of confidence after using the game as a training tool to test strategies and techniques such as card counting that will supposedly give them an edge. Storm King, an academic writer, has an interesting article with a discussion on both Internet gambling and pornography [4].

9.2 – Internet Dating

There are a variety of places on the Internet that advertise opportunities for dating. Many such places have people use a sign on, post a picture, write an essay, and post answers to frequently asked questions. One can also use a database to perform queries and make list of potential dates based on certain criteria. One could use income, religion, or lifestyle as a means of finding a list of people one feels may make potential soul-mates. However; after reading a variety of postings on the Internet, I get the impression many married people represent themselves as single which can cause an unknowing single person into an adulterous situation. Any situation where one partner in the relationship is married has the potential of resulting in violence from a jealous spouse and should be avoided.In order to avoid potential litigation some dating sites have been proactive by asking members to sign a legal paper that states they are not married. There are a few Internet dating websites that warn it is a felony for a person who has taken an oath that they are single, when in fact they are actually married, to date a single member. Apparently there is a real problem with people using the anonymousness of the communication medium to check for extra marital opportunities on the Internet.

Some informal postings on the Internet inform that many young women from Eastern Europe are posting their picture and looking to use the Internet dating sites as a means of finding a husband in the United States or other western nation. Any person considering such international relationships would be advised to go to the FBI or CIA website and read about people-trafficking and mail order brides. Many men engaging in such a practice most likely do not understand the culture, language, and history of the woman they seek to date. Such a relationship starts with great barriers in economic disparity as well as language and culture. Women from Eastern Europe have most probably formed their thoughts and opinions of America from movies and television which is an inaccurate preconception. It would seem that such Internet dating sits could also be promoting great disappointment for both people.

Considering all the risks of Internet dating, the potential losses appear larger than the gains. If you do have relatives in your home such as those in "Keeping Up Appearances", who use your computer, than you may want to consider blocking online dating sites and encourage realistic social relationships in their local community.

9.2.1 – Chat rooms
Some Internet service providers have an interface that allows anyone to use what is commonly known as a chat room to type to people. Chat rooms can be very useful and allow people with special interests like Corvair car clubs to swap automobile parts and discuss complicated procedures such as changing the transmission.

However, chat rooms have also allowed men to portray themselves as much younger and have inappropriate conversations with girls below the age of 18. It is important to be able to verify the age and gender of the other party, because the unfortunate part is that these mediums are used to lure minors into sexual situations with non minors which is illegal and can cause untold emotional harm and distress.

I took a computer forensics class that was taught by a police detective and was shocked to learn that some men start by talking to girls on the chat room and then move to video conferencing on Netmeeting. The detective said there have been occasions where the men ask the underage girls to flash some skin on the webcam. If I were a parent, I would keep the computer in the living room where my kids could be supervised and only use the webcam for approved video conferences with known family and friends.

9.3 – Internet Cigarette Purchases
Many people complain that cigarettes can be ordered from various Internet sources often representing themselves as Indian reservations. Are they really reservations? Could minors purchase cigarettes this way? What about the local governments being denied legitimate tax money needed for public projects? There a lot of unanswered questions with this and a lot of potential for harm. Please be aware of your local laws regarding cigarette purchasing.

9.4 – Buying Drugs on the Internet
I took a very informative class on computer forensics a few years ago. It was excellent and taught by two computer crime detectives that I have great respect for. We examined readings

and Internet articles about people buying illegal drugs from overseas and using the standard package carriers to deliver it. I could not believe people would have the audacity to do such a thing. One thing about the reading that stuck in my mind was the ridiculousness of a story about a man in the traditional mafia that talked about how the outsourcing of the drug business really hit American drug dealers just as outsourcing to India has hit computer programmers. He then said it was getting harder to earn a good living as an American criminal because of foreign competition.

9.5 – People Review The Website Surfer

I was reading "The World is Flat" by N.Y. Times Thomas Friedman. It is a good book and gives one an insight into how various entities including paramilitary organizations use the Internet. When it comes to the bad guys, he says that Al-Queda really utilizes computer technology and uses the Internet to publish videos of beheadings and other activities. Rebels in the Chechnya Republic even published bank accounts where supporters can deposit money. The Internet can also put terrorists and sympathizers with money together. It is not surprising to learn there are many terrorist websites where an alternate viewpoint is put across in order to try to win new recruits to their cause. I was surprised that there is a website log file that the terrorists survey to see who is viewing their website. The data is mined and the visitor who seems ultra interested, and could potentially serve the organization and its work, are subsequently contacted [5].

Perhaps you are wondering how you can be identified. Well the website administrator just gets the IP numbers out of the log and puts in the IP number in one of the boxes at www.samspade.org or another similar website. Often a person's name address, phone number, email, and every other thing is visible. It makes it real easy to identify readers: who they are, and where they live. You can also use that information in a google search to get more information. It is frightening to many people how much information about you, and what your surfing habits are, is out there. If you get a special tool, all the websites you view are in a file in the Windows Operating system called index.dat. Some people such as private investigators make an excellent living on collecting, organizing, and reporting on public information.

9.6. – Purchasing Things Online

I purchased an antique telephone in March of 2005 on a famous online auction site. Then I sent a United States money order for $75.00. The price was fair and the phone was a 100 year old phone from Canada. I was buying it for a relative who liked the old model because it was good for their hearing problem. I got a myriad of excuses for sixty days such as, "I live in a rural area and it takes an hour to drive to the bank, I will get to the bank next week because of the snow and dirt roads." Well after 60 days you have no recourse with the auction house. I went to my local postmaster and there is little we can do because Canada is a foreign country. The postmaster told me I could go there to Canada and file a complaint and he told me how his son was also ripped off buying things outside the United States. There are nice websites for the Federal Trade Commission where you can report such things. A lot can be done for such matters within the USA but when it crosses the border, you are basically on your own. I am mentioning this because there are many items outside the USA that appear to good to be true and they probably are. My phone that I paid for has probably been sold many times. I had a hard time getting rid of my account at the auction site but it happened after 2 weeks. I have bought many things within the United States without a problem using the Internet.

9.7 – The Family Computer

I think it is a good idea to have the family computer in a secure area and each person who uses it has a bios password. Each person who will use the computer should have a windows account and their own directory for files. They should have their own email account. Each person should be able to access only their documents. The rules for behavior should be established by the person who owns the computer. Everyone should know their right or no right to privacy and agree to it. If the owner uses a forensic tool to check where people go on the Internet or check temp files for remnants of chat room sessions, everyone should be informed ahead of time and agree to it. There are a lot of legal issues to consider and it is worth a trip to the family legal advisor since I am not qualified to give legal advice. This paragraph was only to give you ideas.

REFERENCES

1. Chiu, S., Lee, J., Huang, D., (2004), "Video Game Addiction in Children and Teenagers in Taiwan", Cyberpsychology and Behavior, Volume 7, Number 5, Mary Ann Liebert, Inc., Page 571-581, ISSN: 1094-9313
2. Miller, S., (2002),"Milwaukee Sentinel", March 30,2002
3. Doherty, E., Stephenson, G., (2005),"Computer Recreation for Everyone", ISBN 1-4208-2239-X, Authorhouse Publishing, Indiana, Page 149
4. King, S., (1999),"Internet Gambling and Pornography: Illustrative Examples of the Pschological Consequences
5. Friedman, T., (2005), "The World is Flat", N.Y, N.Y., ISBN 0-374-29288-4, Page 433-4

Chapter 10 –
Information Warfare and Countermeasures

10.0 – Introduction

There is a lot of interest about various types of networks in both the private and public sector. This chapter is an attempt to give people a look into various measures that the United States military and various other agencies use to detect electronic communications and signals about matters concerning national security over electronic telecommunications networks and in the air. Then we will look at a variety of agencies and military technologies that help keep America safe. We will also look at a variety of perceptions about technology that influence behavior and may ultimately affect national security.

10.1 The United States Army Military Intelligence and Networks

A retired general named Claudia Kennedy, says in her book that the United States Army is a peace keeping organization composed of many elements including military intelligence (MI). It is my personal opinion that MI is a good area for young patriotic Americans who are interested in networking, mathematics, and electronics. It offers a challenging career that takes them around the world protecting American interests and exporting global security. General Claudia Kennedy was a Lieutenant General, three star general, who spent the majority of her career in this area, namely M.I. [1]. U.S. Army Military Intelligence personnel will monitor wireless communications in the forms of radio, telephony, and various electromagnetic signals on the battlefield to determine where the enemy is, what the enemy is doing, and plans to do. MI may also use various types of computers with fast processors to aid it in decryption where large numbers of permutations of characters must be run. Decryption is generally considered by network security professionals as the collection of scrambled signals and the deciphering of them using various permutations of characters, to produce understandable speech or text.

MI also uses various sensor networks to collect the wide array of electromagnetic signals on the battlefield to identify enemy equipment and its position on the battlefield [1]. Such information can be input to a computer and gives the commanders a single operational picture of the battlefield with all friendly and enemy forces labeled on the map as with the Force XXI Battle Command, Brigade-and-Below (FBCB2). You can learn more about FCBC2 on the DARPA website. FCBC2 system we will discuss shortly. The detection and decryption of enemy signals allow United States military commanders to have the best information to what the enemy will do. It is my opinion that the US military uses expensive systems to pinpoint the enemy forces and friendly forces so as to reduce injuries to foreign civilians and surrounding buildings known as (collateral damage) when engaging in combat.

A video that was created by Northup Grumman and distributed to the public at the New Jersey Homeland Security Conference at Fort Monmouth on June 7, 2004 in NJ described the FCBC2 system. The video showed a computer hardware and software networked system that was used in Operation Iraqi Freedom and in Operation Enduring Freedom in Afghanistan. The system used a variety of sensors and a communication satellite. FCBC2 allowed soldiers and commanders complete situational awareness of all forces and strengths on the battlefield. It even allowed real time communication and mapping of all units on the battlefield and in violent sandstorms so no time was lost during bad weather. The video also said FCBC2 is a powerful network system that allows text messaging and the placing of graphics on a map. Coalition forces, United States forces, and the Pentagon were all communicating, coordinating resources, and planning where to stop the enemy as they used an accurate real time map. Many of these maps were shown on laptop screens in Humvees. FCBC2 is also credited with saving many lives by reducing the chances of friendly fire and fratricide. The FCBC2 Blue Force Tracking is also being integrated with the United States Air Force J-Stars program for more capability with the Air Force. Hand held units are being developed for land forces not in a vehicle [2].

The video shows that Northup Grumman is a major player in developing military network systems. I think that a young woman or man who is interested in developing expensive complex systems such as FCBC2 might consider reading the Northup Grumman website and apply for a position there as a programmer, engineer, or technician. It appears that there will be a need for constant development of sophisticated networked military systems for many years to come especially since there appears to be so much instability in various parts of the world.

10.1.1 – Hacking Military Networks

The idea of hacking into the Pentagon and controlling a United States asset such as a missile, by hackers or enemy forces, was introduced in the 1983 movie "War Games" starring movie actor Matthew Broderick. I remember it touched a nerve with the American public who were seeing a military that was being transformed to higher levels of automation and connectivity through various wired and wireless telecommunication / computer networks – something that President Reagan was thinking of doing in real life with his 'Star Wars' initiative. The idea of a technically savvy rogue opponent acting big by harnessing the power of the United States military was horrible and there was a lot of concern about network security after that movie. The idea was not so far fetched because there was a military exercise where an Air Force officer in a hotel room in the USA was able to enter a Navy network and disturb the navigation data of a ship at sea which could have put the large ship off course. A real Navy incident happened some years ago when 2/3 of the source code for a satellite and missile guidance system was stolen from a Washington D.C. Research Facility [3].

Another alarming fact is that 95% of military communications run through civilian phones lines which could potentially be tapped by a rogue employee. The Department of Defense also has its networks probed by hackers or potential terrorists about 250,000 times per year and every probe must be investigated [3]. There is gossip among the public in the U.K. that the SAS in Britain allegedly use a secret proprietary global satellite system for all their communications, ensuring total anonymity.

10.1.2 – More American Information Security Specialists are Needed

Some computer forensics and network experts such as John Vacca, a former police officer and author of Computer Forensics, state that a large scale cyberattack is imminent. He also states that members of terrorist groups such as Hezbollah have people in it who were educated in American and United Kingdom universities. Some of these western educated people may even be capable of developing such a large scale 9-11 attack on the network against digital assets. Digital assets could be our financial network, or the network controlling the power grid that is used to regulate electricity going to power lights, hospitals, homes, and anything else requiring electricity. I would like to encourage American youth to go into careers that strengthen our critical infrastructure known as Cyberspace. Such careers can be in either the public or private sector.

There is a plethora of literature that suggests young American women are not encouraged enough to enter careers in science and engineering. That is practically half of the United States population. Women have for years been a underutilized force in American society and America only had its first woman three star general in the 1990s [1]. Thomas Friedman, author of "The World is Flat" also indicates concern throughout his book that American girls are being discouraged by their parents from going into computer science because it offers a poor life. I feel it is important to encourage young women to become computer scientists, engineers, and mathematics majors because they are an intelligent resource that can greatly contribute to developing new network architectures, policies, and encryption algorithms to protect our nation's networks.

Parents' perceptions of a "poor life" are also echoed sometimes in editorials in the newspapers. Thomas Friedman's book implies that a poor life means long hours and constant retraining for modest pay. Friedman states that the "flattening of the world" due to high quality broadband Internet, cheap long distance telephone rates, and excellent video conferencing has turned computer work into a commodity that can be outsourced to places where labor is cheap and where the cost of living is much less expensive. The parents of many young people tell me they see computer work traveling around different developing nations, formerly known as "Third World Countries" until it reaches the place with the people who will work the longest hours for the least pay. This cannot bode well for quality assurance or security as a whole.

I will now demonstrate one example of the migration of computer work from Thomas Friedman's book. Friedman speaks of some data entry and database work that was outsourced to Cambodia because they could get lower wage workers than India. I told you Thomas Freidman's economic explanation of why computer work has been outsourced and why this commodity can command a low wage. Now I will tell you from my observations of the private and public sector why I feel many American parents may discourage their daughters from studying computer science. When it comes to programming for example, one has to constantly learn new programming paradigms that are only useful for short periods of time and it takes a lot of time and training and practice to be proficient. For example, years ago, I learned visual basic 6.0 which took considerable time and effort. Then visual basic .NET came out and it was completely different and took a lot of time to become proficient with. However; being proficient with the old version of visual basic provided little help with the new version. It is like constantly starting over.

I have experience as a computer professional in industry, the educational sector, and the government sector. I also speak to many people in all sectors and read trade journals. My opinion is based on personal experience coupled with what I learn talking to other information technology professionals I speak to in the United States and the United Kingdom. The sentiment commonly expressed is that too often and in too short a time-span you are often expected to produce work right away with a new programming language that a university or workplace selects. One is quickly expected to be an expert programmer to teach students in a school environment or write programs quickly and efficiently in private industry. Budgets and time constraints rarely allow the American or U.K. information technology worker or professor sufficient time to go to a training facility for a week to learn a new programming platform such as .NET. The time to achieve proficiency is often required to be done in your own time after work.

My years of experience with the previous version of visual basic 6 did not help me much with the .NET version and I will probably never use visual basic 6.0 again. I am very fortunate to presently work at a place where I receive ample computer forensic and network security training and have resources available to publish and attend conferences. I never discussed this aspect of computing but was fortunate to have excellent leadership from one of my previous employers who asked me to read a book called, "The Social Life of Information" by John Seely Brown and Paul Duguid. It was published by Harvard Business Press in 2002. I was then asked to discuss it on a panel with other engineering professors and computer science students from foreign countries.

There was a large audience and the book voiced all the concerns I previously mentioned and other concerns I thought, but did not dare voice. The book was excellent and provided discussion by students at my university and others nearby. Three international students from the Saudi Arabian peninsula heard of my discussions on the book and decided to speak to me after the talk about their perception of technology and how it would impact their career choices for when they returned home. These students have told me they see the constant changing of programming paradigms and operating systems with no end of rapid change in sight. They echoed the same sentiments of the book and the concerns I voiced. The three I spoke to have all opted for master's degrees in management information systems degrees instead of ending with a bachelor's degree in computer science and programming.

These students expressed an idea that a manager could generally know how a technology worked and not have to be proficient in every detail. Being a manager and having a working knowledge of a technology was doable in a regular workday and allowed a lifestyle of more family time, leisure, and participation in their community. The three men said they would rather manage information technology at companies back home and leave the long hours of ever changing programming to lower paid expatriates of other countries. Is it possible that Arabic nations could have a national security issue with their networks one day if many of their brightest minds opt for a career in management and not in computer science and engineering?

Most computer industry people and academics I have met in the USA will endure very long hours and constant learning while they are still young and establishing a career but most do not consider it a viable option for an entire career. These long days are a combination of doing your regular work as well as learning ever changing programming paradigms and becoming proficient in them. Many people feel that middle aged people need time to raise children, maintain a marriage, and participate in their community. The same rapid changing of programming languages and paradigms appears less in various versions of network operating systems. Therefore many American computer scientists go into other fields where using the computer is only part of one's duties and they can be paid well and still devote more time to their family and community. Many people say that "We work to live, not live to work". Network security policy development and Geographic Information Systems (GIS) are two areas that I feel a computer scientist can retool and excel in.

John Vacca, author of Computer Forensics, is probably aware of this common sentiment. He worries that we need to encourage more Americans to go into computer science, network security, and engineering because we are growing more and more dependent on networks to run our military, life support systems at the hospital, banking and financial houses, and power networks. At the same time we are becoming more and more dependent on these networks, and placing more trust in these networks, while less college age Americans are going into computer science and related fields. In the future, I don't think it would be a good practice if the United States had such a shortage of network security specialists that we had to rely on specialists imported from another country to work on highly confidential military and law enforcement networks.

Thomas Friedman in his book, "The World is Flat" says more and more people in countries outside the USA have their youth studying computer science and engineering. Less Americans are studying computer science and engineering and he says it will become a serious concern for our network dependent country maintaining the level of national security in possibly fifteen years from now. We need to encourage the youth of America to become computer scientists and engineers so that we can maintain a technological edge above other nations and maintain our status as a global leader in security. Such an edge in my opinion should keep developing nations who see our way of life as a threat, from successfully using a Cyberattack to cripple our critical infrastructure in Cyberspace. The Department of Homeland Security has a Cyberspace critical infrastructure protection element to protect our financial, power, military, and law enforcement networks.

Thomas Friedman's book also points out that many American companies and international corporations are relocating to places like Bangalore, India. He also says Bangalore is a beautiful city where one can have a great life with one of these jobs outsourced from America. Thomas further says in his book that we cannot rely on the best and brightest from other lands to fill our jobs as countries such as India and China develop and there exist opportunities for graduating students to have nice jobs and comfortable jobs near their families.

Think tank specialists and policy makers in the United States probably have also felt a need for increasing the number of American students studying information security, information assurance, and computer science. Fortunately there are new programs with the National Science Foundation in partnership with the National Security Agency for increasing the number of American network security professionals through scholarships and grants. There are even grants for developing Information Assurance curriculum at various universities in the USA. However; many academics who have successfully implemented such programs at their universities say it is difficult to navigate all the politics and get all the incumbent people to do their part to implement such programs.

Such information assurance programs already existing at universities also need to be advertised more so young people will take advantage of these programs. Parents need to be made aware of these programs so that they encourage their children to take advantage of them.

10.2 – Information Warfare, Zombies, and the Ping of Death
There are times where people who go to a website don't realize they may be downloading some malware also known as malicious software. Sometimes this software appears to do nothing but will activate on a certain date as John Vacca discusses in his book. The activated software will ping a website such as the FBI server at www.fbi.gov. Each computer that activates on that day is known as a zombie and such computers might be controlled by one person doing a zombie attack. If the FBI server has their ping service turned off, it will not have to handle these requests. However; if the ping service is activated, then the server will get more requests than it can handle and the buffers will fail, as may the server.

10.3 – Intelligence / Law Enforcement Systems
There are certain intelligence gathering systems such as "Echelon" that some newspaper people have reported do exist. However, most likely for security reasons, the United States government does not publish the facts on such systems. It does not mean such systems do not exist but discussing them fully in the public arena could give the bad guys some idea of their capability and might allow them to develop countermeasures to make them less effective. However; the idea of such a vague system may deter some would be criminals from doing bad things, by making them think twice: which is good. A bit like the way the TV series CSI has made would be criminals think twice about how modern DNA and forensics techniques are used to track down perpetrators. I will briefly describe such a system and give sources for you to investigate.

10.3.1 – Echelon
In France, Parliament President Nicole Fontaine said Echelon is a violation of the rights of European Union citizens. However; Echelon was charged as the system used to discover that France was offering bribes to Saudi Arabia in some multi-billion dollar business deals. The Saudis got complaints from America and gave them the deals. The Echelon system supposedly

scans billions of phone calls, email, and faxes per hour. It would seem plausible that certain keywords could be flagged and prioritized for analysts to check. Perhaps certain information that could be important might be directed to various intelligence agencies to investigate in more detail [6].

10.3.2 – Omnivore / Carnivore

A website called "How Stuff Works" [5] has reported that the FBI has a system called Carnivore. The purpose of this system is to help law enforcement officials monitor network traffic, specifically email, to monitor illegal or suspicious activity. The person who might be involved in such suspicious or illegal activity is commonly known as a subject of interest (SOI) [4]. The system supposedly has a component installed at the SOI's ISP which sends all email ASAP to the FBI for analysis. It would appear that Carnivore did not meet the FBI's needs for surveillance since it only handled email and not more new and increasingly popular modes of communication on computers such as Internet Telephony and video conferencing with Netmeeting.

The FBI is reported to have created an improved version of Carnivore called Omnivore in 1997. This version allowed more efficient methods of archiving email and printing it out. However, this too did not seem to meet their needs as more people were using Internet telephony to make free calls over the Internet and videoconference with Netmeeting. It was reported that the FBI came out with a new law enforcement tool called the Dragonware Suite in 1999. This new suite contained three components which are: Packeteer, Coolminer, and Omnivore [5]. Omnivore allowed email to be sent to the FBI, backed up on tape, and printed on paper for analysts to review. Coolminer is reported to be a tool for data mining which means a way of examining text for key phrases or groups of phrases to indicate trends. The last element of Carnivore is the Packeteer, this is said to allow packets of webpages or Internet telephony conversations to be directed from the SOI's ISP to the FBI and reassembled for viewing or listening. Such tools in my opinion should not cause alarm to a public obsessed with privacy since they are used in authorized situations by responsible law enforcement professionals. Many security professionals have said that the public cannot have complete safety and complete privacy at the same time.

10.3.3 – Total Information Awareness

There is a plethora of information on the Internet concerning Total Information Awareness (TIA) so what I am reporting is not classified. You can do a search using Google and find out more than I am mentioning. TIA is reported to be a system that is being developed in cooperation between the Department of Defense and the Defense Advanced Research Projects Agency (DARPA). The system will supposedly collect information from such disparate systems of hotels, credit card agencies, and car rental agencies and allow law enforcement a larger data set to mine and seek clues from. A larger pool of information from more sources should reveal more complex relationships and reveal more clues to catch terrorists much more easily.

10.3.4 – RFCL

The RCFL is an acronym for the "Regional Computer Forensic Labs." There are approximately seven of these labs in the United States. Such labs have digital evidence examiners who are considered by many to be an elite force of law enforcement officials who are both willing and available to provide assistance and expertise to the smaller towns that do not have the resources to adequately investigate crimes that involve computers or networked computers. It is my opinion that RFCLs are necessary because the rapidly changing operating systems and the plethora of new computers entering the public market make it impossible for even large police departments with more computer and network experts to keep up with the demand. The RFCL is probably the brainchild of far sighted policy makers who foresaw the rapid change of information technology and realized there needed to be a centralized repository that other agencies could tap into so. This centralized resource reduces the need for expensive duplication of training and labs around the United States. I feel such resource sharing is necessary if the United States is to manage its national debt wisely.

10.4 – Homeland Security Related Research and Hope for the Future

Americans are worried about security in the 21st century and there is much concern as we have stated. However; there is also much research and development in a variety of Homeland Security related areas that result in usable products for law enforcement, the military, and private security. Channel 50 New Jersey Public News has reported that Rutgers University is organizing partnerships between law enforcement, the military, and various universities through its Rutgers Homeland Security Consortium. Public domain literature from a Homeland Security conference I attended on 26-28 April, 2005 in Boston revealed that Rutgers also has scientists like Nabil Adam who examines semantic graph based knowledge discovery from heterogeneous information sources. I feel such work could help systems like the "Total Information Awareness" better detect relationships among information among disparate systems. Matt Welsh at Harvard University has examined wireless sensor networks for emergency care and disaster response. Both men presented papers at the "Working Together: R&D Partnerships in Homeland Security Conference" in Boston on April 27th and April 28th , 2005 in Boston, Massachusetts. I also attended, representing Fairleigh Dickinson University, and presented a poster at the same conference about unauthorized area networks and discussed a strategy to prevent one. It is the sharing of information, technology, and intra-agency cooperation among scientists, academics, law enforcement, the military, and the defense industry that will help reduce the impact of terrorism and Cyberattacks.

REFERENCES

1. Kennedy, C., (2001),"Generally Speaking", Abridged version for books on tape, Time Warner Audio Books, ISBN 1-58621-175-7
2. FCBC2, Blue Force Tracking DVD, Northup Grumman, DVD Video, 6 minutes, Produced in cooperation with the Brigade Battle Command (Public Domain)
3. Vacca, J., Page 574-5
4. Titel, E., Shinder, D., (2002) "Scene of the Cybercrime Computer Forensics Handbook", Syngress Books, ISBN 1-931836-65-5, Page 304
5. URL http://computer.howstuffworks.com/carnivore1.htm   visited Nov11, 2004
6. Vacca, " ",Pages 387,412,547
7. URL www.fas.org/irp/crs/RL31730.pdf   visited Nov. 11, 2004

Chapter 11 –
A Look at Education PT/FT, Consulting,
Various Career Paths

11.0 - Introduction – A Music Television Video (MTV) in the 1980s featured a stern authoritarian adult figure that approaches a young man, and says, "What are you going to do with your life?" In the video the young man jumps up and says, "I want to rock" and in the rest of the video we see him progress toward a career as a rock star. Well most of you reading this book are probably not going to be a rock star and are looking for something more mundane. If you have made it this far in the book you might be considering a career in network security, computer forensics, private security, or law enforcement, or even having your own computer installation, repair, and security company. You may be considering a career in teaching, being a consultant, or working as a contractor for the Federal government. Perhaps you even thought of doing a stint in the Middle East for big pay. Let's look at a couple examples of real jobs that are often available and theoretical examples of jobs.

11.1 – Being a Computer / Network Security Consultant
I will share a story with you about when I did some private consulting work at a small company from a contact I made when teaching some continuing education classes at a county college for the business community. I hope the story gives you some practical insight into some of the benefits and drawbacks of being a consultant. I must have done something correctly because I worked for them for many years on a part time basis. In the 1990s, I set up their PCs, configured their modems and dialup accounts, installed Microsoft Office, as well as registered a domain, created a website for them, and taught them how to use Microsoft Word with a database to do mailings. The company was in the United States. Its services included hazardous waste cleanup and expert witness work. I was paid well as a computer consultant and had no trouble collecting my money. The work was very interesting but the work was infrequent. I found it was a great bonus but not steady enough to do full time. Though I got great pay, there were no benefits. However; I did not market my services.

You may find being a consultant is the way to go if you market your services correctly, line up enough work to pay the bills, and have a lot of practical experience to draw upon.

If you don't have enough work experience to draw upon, being able to read manuals, follow directions, and knowing the technical support numbers for the products you will install may get you through the work successfully. Some bosses in corporations will tell you college degrees are not really necessary unless their industry regulates the educational qualifications of the consultant. My impression of what was important to some small corporations hiring a consultant was experience and being able to do the job reliably, inexpensively, and quickly. You may also have to know how to use ftp, telnet, web designer tools, and should know Microsoft Windows and some UNIX or Xenix for government customers. It is also very helpful to know MS Office, how to set up and maintain a website, and how to install, repair, and configure a large variety of desktop computers and peripheral devices. In the last year with broadband wireless connectivity being more prevalent among businesses, firewalls and intrusion detection are being requested by increasing numbers of businesses.

Depending on the number of customers that you find, and their security needs which may be regulated by their industry or community, you may find you are arranging high security ISDN leased lines with companies like Verizon and supervising their installation and testing the line quality on the modem. Then you may be setting up IBM CSU/DSUs that act like multipoint modems along those lines for each office on the leased line. These multipoint lines may go to a centralized mainframe in the area for example. You may be working with a contractor who puts in line of sight, point to point satellite dishes that cannot be more that 5 degrees off and connecting the satellite modem to a 3278 IBM control unit and dumb terminals. A computer security professor who has testified as an expert witness in court on a previous occasion told me it was his personal opinion that such setups are nearly impossible for a hacker to break.

You may also purchase personal computers for a client, connect cable modems at their place of business, and be well paid to use MAC address filtering with their router/switch configured only to allow transactions from those machines. Perhaps you will charge $50 per hour and perform a vulnerability assessment by checking physical security, accounts on the machine, perform leak tests, perform penetration tests, and even examine some kind of audit log. It is my opinion that people will hire consultants as temporary employees if they can give them price worthy, reliable service within a set deadline.

11.2 – Being an Expert Witness

I was told by my boss at the toxic waste cleanup company, mentioned above, that they would charge clients approximately $250 per hour in the 1990s for hazardous waste cleanup work. The investigator, who went to the site, collected evidence, created a report, directed a plan of cleanup, was sometimes an expert witness who might to testify on the cleanup or levels of contamination. My boss at the time wanted to expand the business and capitalize on my practical computer expertise but in the 1990s I was working on my master's degree and felt I did not have the credentials to become an expert witness in the simplest case involving computers. People I know who are expert witnesses told me they are often paid as much as a thousand dollars a day on the stand. They must also qualify as an expert through a process called "Voir Dire." [2]

The process called "voir dire" means you need to demonstrate to the court that you understand your area of expertise by answering questions during cross examination by the opposing attorney about the authors in your field, books, formulas, and various theories in your area of expertise. Your education, experience, published papers, and books published will be scrutinized as you are questioned. I believe it would be in your best interest to take a class to prepare you for such an experience.

Fairleigh Dickinson University has a class in the School of Administrative Science called the Forensic Expert which I took in the Spring of 2003. My personal opinion from a student perspective was that it was a great class and I wish the course had been available in the 1990s because I would have taken it. I feel it might have helped me in my career then. The FDU professor for the class I took was an investigator who had testified in court. I also liked his class so much I studied network security with him too. The professor also recommended a book called Testifying in Court by Stanley L. Brodsky [3]. The book alleviated some of my fears about testifying in court.

I just want to restate it would probably be in your best interest to learn the United States Federal Rules of Evidence 701-706 concerning expert witnesses if you wish to work as an expert witness. In this last example concerning consulting, I said that education was perceived by some as not that important but experience and results were important. However, many people in industry feel a college degree and certifications are important and insist on it. In the next section I will talk about the importance of higher education in the form of degrees, credentials, and publishing experience all of which are important as well as essential.

11.3 – United Arab Emirates – 2 Year Contract Professor

I patented a telephone dialer for non-verbal people with physical disabilities along with a bright person from Sharjah and two other bright students from India. The student from Sharjah spoke of the nice university there and the excellent pay that foreigners could earn. I will use this university as an example for well paid overseas teaching work. You may also wish to teach networking and basic computer security at an American style university in English, in Sharjah. The United Arab Emirates (U.A.E.) borders Saudi Arabia. Many American companies have invested there and many people I know who have visited this area say it's considered a nice place to visit and work.

The United Arab Emirates (U.A.E.) was also called the Trucial States when it was British. Some people say Sharjah and Dubai are terrific places to go to experience modern and classic Arabic culture. American businessmen tell me that the Emirates combines the best of the modern world with Arabic culture. Sharjah has beaches and sand dunes where people can enjoy driving dune buggies. Sharjah has souqs or markets as well as many new technologies and buildings [1]. People tell me it is modern and a great place for shopping.

The website for the University of Sharjah leads me to believe it pays competitively but the money you earn goes further because it is tax free and housing and transportation to and from the U.A.E. is generally advertised on their website to be provided by the university. All you need is to have a Ph.D., some teaching experience, and some publications. They give an allowance for children's education too and 60 days leave per year. Please go to the University of Sharjah website and seek more information if you are interested.

The U.A.E. student who patented the phone dialer for the disabled and I once were on TV in the U.A.E. and in the Al Khaleej newspaper three times which is distributed throughout the United Arab Emirates. Each time, we showed assistive technology that used computers and telephone networks to allow handicapped people to communicate in Arabic, English, and Chinese. These stories were not reprints of American stories or TV. The student told me there was some interest from people throughout the U.A.E, including students, for creating applications to help the disabled communicate, recreate, and improve their lives.

It is my personal opinion that it is always important to find out by reading the website or by direct contact if the university you wish to teach at supports or encourages the kind of research you do. It is also good to search Google for some of the faculty names and see what kind of articles they publish and determine their research interests. Their research interests may be in an area that you wish to branch off into. Working there might create new opportunities for you while collaborating on projects with them. If you read the website for visiting scholars and employment opportunities, you will see some universities require visiting contract professors to supervise some master and doctoral thesis students in a certain areas of computing or even specialized areas within network security. Sometimes university administrators feel the visiting professor often has less value to the university and students if he or she cannot mentor graduate students doing research and developing a thesis.

11.3.1 – University Professor in Hong Kong

In May 1998, I visited the City University of Hong Kong to demonstrate some brain computer interface research I was doing while obtaining my doctorate. There were many American and British academics there and at the Hong Kong Baptist University. I was amazed at the salaries they commanded. They also received housing from the University.

I was told by academics from around the world that Hong Kong academics were the highest paid academics in the world and only had to pay a flat 10% income tax for money earned that year. In the late 1990s and early 2000s, it was not uncommon to see universities advertising faculty positions in the Communications of the ACM Career Opportunities section for US$100K and upwards. I was told by some academics that housing was often provided without cost. Computer scientists hired for faculty positions would teach classes, do research and development, and publish in areas such as human computer interaction (HCI), network security, or engineering. Some academics said faculty was often expected to partner with local companies on projects.

Academics who were familiar with international pay scales told me the net pay was much higher than Sharjah and the Middle East but I felt from talking to academics in Hong Kong that there was a lot more pressure to perform and one could burn out if one was not careful. Hong Kong appeared to me to be a nice place to visit and I felt relatively safe there in 1998. The underground trains, ferries, and cable cars made travel quick and easy. I felt the shopping was amazing and there were great places to hike near Beacon Hill and the outskirts of the city. There were many historical sites and first class places to eat lunch, like the restaurant in the Hotel Peninsula. However; one should look at The United States State Department website to get more information on travel advisories for any foreign country and possibly contact the American Embassy there if one is seriously considering a work assignment outside the USA.

11.3.1.5 – Computer Security / Computer Application Teacher – Cruise Ship

A fellow professor retired a few years ago and found a position as a computer instructor on a cruise ship. He told me he was given a salary of approximately US$28,000 per 6 months and accommodation for he and his wife was provided. The man had to teach on board classes a few times a week on all the applications of Microsoft Office and perhaps a basic network security class. It sounded appealing to many because of the ample leisure time and all the lovely Caribbean islands they visited.

11.3.2 – Network Security Class – Adjunct Professor – USA College or University

I have been an adjunct professor at the both the community college and four year college in the United States. I have known many adjuncts at a variety of different colleges and universities over the years. I am giving you my opinion. It is only an opinion and not fact. Most adjunct professors I met at the two year college had a four year degree while most university adjuncts who teach undergraduate and graduate classes have at least a master's degree. Most of these schools pay US$2500 - US$3000 per class. I feel that a person with a government pension from a 20 year job and who also has a spouse with a full time job with benefits can afford to work for low pay for the joy of teaching.

The adjunct professor is a great job for the person who likes to teach network security basics, computer applications, or anything on private security in the criminal justice departments. Most adjunct teachers teach for the love of teaching and like people. They draw on their years of experience in law enforcement or private industry, and tend to be more liked by the students because they are in my opinion perceived as having a practical approach to the subject as opposed to the full time academics with doctoral degrees. Students will often like to speak to the adjunct professor about career opportunities because they often have numerous contacts from their years in industry. Students may also seek career advice from the adjunct professor because of their close ties to industry and feel that their insights are quite relevant.

11.3.4 – Full Time Professorship USA – Network Security

I have worked as a full time professor in a tenure track. I have worked previously in a non-tenure track professorship at another school. I have also worked as an adjunct professor and teaching assistant. I have also visited schools and worked on projects in China and England. I have known a lot of professors and have seen many academic institutions around the world. I will now talk generally about being an academic in the USA.

There are two types of full time professorships in the United States. Both types now require a doctorate due to increasing standards of education. The good points about both professorships are that their own children can often go to school for free in the school they are employed in. In fact if you hold any full time job with the university, even maintenance, your children's tuition is free. However, you must pay for lab fees and books. Some universities are in a pool of academic universities so any professor's children can go to any other school in the pool and get free tuition.

Let us first discuss the non-tenure track professor. Many professors say it is much less stressful because there is less pressure to publish books and academic papers but there is often the same expectation for academic committee work. The down side is that at some colleges, there is a limit to your term of service as an employee since you are on the non-tenure track. Often you need to teach 12-15 credits per semester with a class being 3 credits.

Tenure track professorships at many universities mean that when you are hired, you are in a tenure track. Most professors I spoke to about tenure at various universities around the world agree that there are many milestones you have to achieve to be rehired back each year. One has to show volunteer service to a department, division within a university, and the university itself. One also to demonstrate volunteer service to the community, continued education, and publishing books, academic articles, or both. You have to teach 12-15 credits and do a lot of committee work. You will have a review each year and hopefully your contract will be renewed for another 10 month contract. After 5-8 years, depending on the university, a professor will be reviewed by a tenure committee.

Tenure committees are convened at most schools annually and the candidate is measured against a criteria sheet. Tenure is considered by many to be a form of job security but it is also for reasons of academic freedom, too. A no-vote means your tenure is not renewed and must find employment elsewhere. It is my opinion that the tenure track faculty position can offer the university professor a good life and ample opportunities to publish, grow intellectually, travel, meet students from all walks of life, and do fulfilling research.

An old academic in England once told me that the tenure track was a bit like being an apprentice in the Middle Ages. The apprentice studies with the master for many years and performs a lot of the menial tasks too. Either party can separate but there is a point where the master makes a commitment and bestows the title of master of that profession on the apprentice; who then becomes a master, himself. I find that a simple analogy is a better explanation for someone unfamiliar with the education system.

John Jay is an educational institution in Manhattan. It has a computer forensics course. I would encourage anyone who was a digital examiner for a police department with at least a master's degree to apply there for a teaching post. I believe a doctorate is preferred but it is best to contact them.

11.4 – Military Employment for the College Student
You may consider joining the Army National Guard, or joining the Army Reserve Officer Training Core (ROTC) when attending college. There was once a program called simultaneous membership (SMP) in the 1980s where a person could be in the National Guard during college and do their weekend or two per month with the Guard and two weeks in the summer while also being in Army ROTC. After finishing college, I believe you were a first Lieutenan,t as opposed to being a second lieutenant. Then you might choose a military career such as military intelligence, computer network specialist, or one of the many other occupations that work with military and networks.

It is my opinion that the advantage of this is that you can get a security clearance at a young age and get training and experience on high technology networks. Then after four years of college ROTC, and four years of active duty, you could move into a full time civilian career while still remaining a part time soldier and get valuable training that could help you out in your civilian career. It is also more difficult to get a security clearance when you are 40 or 50 because the authorities must investigate all that time in between. It is much easier if the investigators find that you have big blocks of police and military time.

11.5 – Computer Forensic Specialist or Digital Examiner

You can also become a private industry computer forensic specialist. A young man who was a student of mine was hired in this area and said it is a good career because he gets well paid and the work is less complicated than digital examiners in the public sector. The private sector employees sign policies that give the corporation broad powers for the time they are using computers at work. This means that if you are part of an incident response team, the authorized requestor (AR) at your workplace will tell you to perform a computer investigation on a particular computer. There is no lengthy complex process involving a judge, affidavit, and search warrant.

It is my opinion that the corporate computer investigator is not concerned with all the complex legal issues like exigency, probable cause, and the Fourth Amendment that the law enforcement professional is concerned with. The private industry computer investigator who gets authorization from the AR can basically cordon off an area and collect evidence and then remove the necessary evidence which could potentially include the computer and all associated peripheral devices, media, modems, answering machines, and notebooks that may hold clues in the investigation. The AR can authorize an investigation based on a policy violation or a potential criminal violation.

It is my opinion from reading books and speaking to corporate IT professionals that most offenses will probably be policy violations and not have the severity of crime that police deal with. A digital examiner told me 95% of his cases are Windows operating systems and Intel processors. Digital examiners in small companies usually learn how to search Microsoft Windows desktop systems with Intel processors. They may go for training for tools such as Encase or Forensic Toolkit (FTK). I feel it is really good to have a specialty such as Personal Data Assistants (PDAs), or cell phones because there are numerous cell phones and PDAs used by the general population which could be used in a crime. I feel with the simple law of supply and demand that if there is a supply of criminals using cell phones and PDAs, then there should be a demand for PDA and cell phone investigators.

There is a lot of training available for computer forensics and I feel from talking to many graduates that there are a lot of quality programs. I obtained a credential as a PDA Examiner from Paraben because the class time was convenient with my work schedule but as I want to point out, other places could have provided such training. I receive no compensation from mentioning them. I felt the education was reasonably priced as was the toolkit. I was happy that the toolkit and software I practiced with in class was mine to keep, after I became familiar with it. My training also took place in a real computer forensic police lab and many of the units we used in class were either donated or seized.

My teacher did real forensics work for law enforcement and there was a lot of practice using the software and collecting evidence and making reports just as if I was going to go to court for real.

I feel that anyone who considers going into computer forensics in law enforcement should obtain a good knowledge of the law and understand the Fourth Amendment, Digital Evidence Search and Seizure Laws for their jurisdiction, and understand as well as be able to apply concepts such as probable cause, plain view, and exigency so they know if they can legally search and seize digital evidence. When things are done incorrectly, bad people may be acquitted by the legal system due to a technicality. I feel it is an important responsibility to society to be a competent expert so justice is dispensed properly and fairly.

It is my opinion from talking to computer forensics professionals in law enforcement that anyone going into computer forensics in law enforcement needs to be mentally tough. I feel that because they may work on a case with some really awful sex crimes or serial murders. Some of the people doing these horrible crimes may document their crime in pictures and reports and law enforcement digital examiners will have to read such accounts in an investigation. If the computer user was a heroin drug user and dealer who used the computer to record sales and make contacts, some examiners may even have to wear gloves when collecting evidence at the crime scene because of needles and HIV tainted blood on machines or at the crime scene. It may be too much psychologically for some people to handle. I understand that there is a rigorous interview process to select the best person for the job.

If you work in a bigger department on a larger police station perhaps you might chose to work on a less gruesome crime such as theft. On the positive side, you would be investigating cases and helping bring bad characters to justice and thus keeping society safe by helping put such people in prison. I have great respect for the law enforcement professionals who deal with these crimes and stay mentally fit.

11.6 – Security Policy Development

Perhaps you are not a "hands on person" and cannot plug in a cable or can't identify a router from a hub but you understand the law and the concepts of security. You may be the perfect person for writing security polices or updating existing ones. Whenever new legislation like HIPAA or the Sarbanes Oxley Act appears, all organizations need help to know how to apply these amendments to their own company policy and then how to implement them in procedures.

11.7 – Internal Auditing

There are many terrific courses to learn auditing but I found it interesting to see a credential for ethical hacking besides the SANS group so I thought I'd mention it. I get no compensation for mentioning the following company. There is a 5 Day Certified Ethical Hacker course available from Data Safe Services for example in Whippany, New Jersey. Your company might send you to this and perhaps start you off as an internal auditor checking the vulnerabilities from inside and outside your organization. Internal Auditors check security logs, check vulnerabilities, and make sure that policy and procedures are being followed and everything is compliant with industry regulation. Internal auditing may be a nice safe career for you.

11.8 – Disaster Recovery Personnel

You may work for a company that is growing larger and needs a risk management department. Then they may realize they also need someone to write a disaster recovery plan. This means you could be selected to design a plan to move phone networks, computer networks, people, and equipment to another site and restart operations. This could be because of flooding, terrorism, fire, or earthquake. Depending on resources and the type of industry you are in, you may also get the permission to create a "hot site" with everything ready to go at a mirrored location. A "hot site" has every transaction and record mirrored at the other site. Every computer, phone line, and network connection is set up an active at the mirrored site. In case of emergency, the workers only need to get a call and can report to the mirrored site and start working with no time lost. It really is ensuring against disaster, but often this kind of redundant facility is considered to be an expensive exercise – until the day of the disaster: no-one knows what is just around the corner, and it is better to be prepared for just about any event. Just ask anyone who has experienced such a scenario. It is often said that 90% of all businesses that are hit with a major disaster go out of business. Perhaps your company will create a disaster recovery plan and implement it so it is one of the 10%. Jacobs et. Al. discusses the hot site in the SSCP preparation book [4].

11.9 – Mom and Pop Computer Store / Installation / Training / Security

When I lived in an urban area, I often walked to a type of store known as a mom and pop store to buy groceries, the newspaper, simple electronics, and articles of daily living. Many of the store owners were a husband and wife team who told me they liked having a business together and involving their kids in the business. They were there together sometimes 12 hours a day and then would go home together. Sometimes a relative would come in and work there until late. This kind of store gets a lot of people who like to come in off the street, talk, and maybe buy something because it is local and convenient.

If you really enjoy togetherness, perhaps you and your wife may want to have a mom and pop computer store on a side street or a little storefront on Main Street with a couple low cost computers, and some disks, router / switches, and commonly used software and parts on hand. One person can mind the store while the other makes a house call to install software, hardware, or set up a router / switch with the MAC address to only accept transactions from a certain machine. Perhaps you create a custom low cost machine for other customers. You may run a small class or do private tutoring. Your business is kind of a jack of all trades.

You may even charge for phone support. If your mom and pop store can hire someone to help with the language of the ethnic neighborhood you are in, that is even better. Perhaps your neighborhood has a lot of Spanish, Chinese, or Arabic language speakers like many big cities do. If your store can help these people in their language to purchase an affordable computer, connect to the Internet, and communicate with loved ones in the old country, then you have a specialty market. Sometimes senior citizens in ethnic neighborhoods only speak a language other than English and may not drive or want to carry heavy or bulky boxes on a bus. Many such seniors may be happy to go to a trusted person like you, who are nearby, and can provide parts, service, and training in their language.

11.9.5 – Private Investigation

Perhaps you were a policeman and retired. You probably have valuable expertise in report writing, interviewing people, and investigation. You may want to take some classes in computer forensics such as the ones at FDU's School of Administrative Science, http://sas.fdu.edu or at John Jay in Manhattan. You may also want to take a distance learning course from Thompson Education in private investigation. Then afterwards, Thompson Education will give you a kit that helps you get an internship with a private investigator where you live. Private investigation is a wide field and one could devote a whole book to it. It may include many specialties such as going to the courthouse for people and looking up records, to doing computer searches on commercial databases, or helping parents see what Internet sites their children were looking at on the computer. A person could work for a licensed private investigator that was part of a licensed agency. The requirements are very different in many states so it is best to ask the State Police in the state that you live in. Steven Kerry Brown has a book on Private Investigating, ISBN 0-02-864399-2. The book is easy to read and gives you a look into private investigating.

11.9.6 – Corporate Job – Security Devices

Perhaps you will join an organization such as American Society Industrial Security (ASIS) International. There are many good organizations that exist for security but I will mention ASIS International because I am familiar with them. You can go to monthly meetings, meet security professionals working in private industry, government, and academia. You may then seek out the requirements for membership and also seek to obtain a membership if you feel you would benefit by it. It is my opinion that ASIS is a good place to network and find out about local jobs and discuss future hiring trends in the security sector in general with people who can form a more accurate opinion on the topic than I can. Such meetings are often attended by private detectives, private security agency presidents, network security professionals, and a variety of government security professionals from agencies such as the F.B.I. and United States Customs. Sometimes people from companies that make access control badges or Smartcards, for example will be at the ASIS meeting. You may be impressed with their product enough that you wish to seek employment in that company for sales, installation, or research and development.

11.9.7 – Conclusion

If you have an interest in working in education, private industry, or government, then it is my opinion that you really need to network with as many security professionals as possible in government, private industry, and academia. You might find it useful to talk about the type of work available and what areas of the security industry are needed where you live. I feel you could possibly benefit by examining your interests, strengths, weaknesses, ability to focus on details, report writing skills, and decide if you wish to travel or stay at home in your present community. Are you willing to relocate? You need to ask yourself if you want to teach, do research and development, sell products, or install security products and configure them. Can you learn new technologies quickly? Do you have the courage to work on cases that contain offensive material and testify in court? In the end, you will have to live with your choice so please chose well.

REFERENCES

1. Insight Guide, (1998),"Oman and the UAE", ISBN 0-88729-287-9, APA Publications part of the Langenscheidt Publishing Group.
2. Smith, F., Bace., R., (2003), "A Guide to Forensic Testimony", Published by Addison and Wesley, Mass., ISBN 0-201-75279-4, Pages 8,9,276
3. Brodsky, S., (2001),"Testifying in Court, Guidelines and Maxims for the Expert Witness", ISBN 1-55798-128-0, Published by the APA, Washington D.C.
4. Jacobs, J., Clemmer, L., Dalton, M., Posluns, J., (2003)," SSCP, Systems Security Practitioner Study Guide, Syngress Publishing, ISBN 1-931836-80-9, Page 279

Chapter 12 –
A Look Into Cybercrime, Viruses, and Things in Bad Taste

12.0 – Introduction

My lay civilian opinion is that Cybercriminals are basically using the Internet, commonly known as Cyberspace, to commit crimes. It is also my opinion that Cybercrime can be committed anytime there is a victim, taken advantage of by a person who transgresses the legal system where the crime took place, where criminal intent is the sole object. What makes it difficult to detect is that jurisdictions of various countries are often crossed. I could for example be in New Jersey and telnet to a computer in Amsterdam and then telnet to a computer in Addis Ababa through to a computer in Sri Lanka, and through to a computer in Canada to steal some documents. Whose laws were broken? What about the fact that the source and destination are different countries and the control signal to take the document passed through countries that may not have developed Cyber law yet? What about countries not friendly to each other? Will they cooperate in an investigation? These are all complex issues that need to be resolved if the people of the world are to deal with an exponential increase in international Cybercrime and international terrorism. This chapter will look at various types of Cybercrime and the motivations for such crimes and some strategies to prevent it. We will start with a more common simple nuisance crime such as one committed by a person who first writes a virus which then passes along from country to country, destroying innocent people's data.

12.1 – Introduction to Computer Viruses

I taught a class on introduction to computer applications to a group of adults at a community college in the early to mid 1990s. A grandmother was afraid to touch the computer but seemed really determined to be in my course. She was very upset. I finally asked what the issue was. She told the class she wanted to learn how to use the computer to keep up with her youngest grandson who had a computer at her house. However; she was afraid to use the college computer because she was afraid of catching a computer virus herself, possibly put there by a malicious person. The class had a really good laugh and I had to calm the class down and explain that computer viruses cannot be transmitted to humans. I explained that the only virus she might get from the computer was from a cold virus. Some students unfortunately came to class all medicated up with cold medicine but still had runny noses, wiped their hands on their pants, and typed at the computer.

The grandmother realized from the laughter that her idea of her personally catching a computer virus was ridiculous and this experience did much to alleviate her fear more than my personal reassurances. I also explained to the class that her fear was valid and real because there are a great many misconceptions held by the general public about computer viruses, and that when someone genuinely fears they may have an unknown virus, and subsequently become sick, especially in their 80s, it is often very difficult to recover. Many people in the class could understand her viewpoint and she went on to be one of the best students in the class because she wanted to understand the computer that her little grandson was using and the kinds of trouble he could get into and even the kinds of risks that her computer was exposed to when connecting to bulletin boards. She was thinking about protecting her grandson, the computer, and the personal documents on her computer. She had a clear security perspective even back then when few people even thought of such things.

There are various definitions for computer virus' in different computer books and some definitions are better than others. However; I like the simple definition of Shinder and Tittel. They say, "A computer virus is a program that causes an unwanted and often destructive result when run ." [1] Viruses are often spread by floppy diskettes and the virus' is passed when the disk is accessed by the desktop. A virus can also be passed via email attachments throughout the world. In the late 1980s and early 1990s, it was general practice for people to often swap floppy disks or copy software illegally, resulting in all kinds of floppy diskettes being past from computer to computer at work, civic groups, or between friends.

You may ask what is the motivation for creating a virus? Is it always evil? Why would someone waste their time making a program that causes so much grief? Let us now look at a phenomenon of economics, involving the revenue lost from people illegally copying software, and how a virus which played a part in that situation might have knowingly taught people a lesson why not to copy software. I am not condoning the situation but am speculating on why it might have been done. We will now closely examine the economics, politics, mechanics, and prevention of such viruses and use a famous event that happened in 1986 [2].

Let us say for example that an American company hires workers to create a software package for calculating spreadsheets and do accounting work. It is a significant investment in people to program these computers. It is a substantial risk to a company that is investing its capital in people's pay and health plans, utilities, rent, and not engaging in other economic activity. If you buy a computer software product licensed to a single user and one machine, you're purchasing a program to use, and giving a return on the investment originally made by that company. However, when someone illegally copies software for a friend, the friend has the use of that program but has not paid for it. Some say software piracy is a crime because it is stealing: others will argue it is not a crime because the original copy still remains the possession of the owner.

Freeware is software that is made by hobbyists to copy and distribute it freely. There is also shareware that is made for people to copy and distribute freely but if you use it, there is a mechanism in it that reminds you to submit a payment for its use. We are not too concerned with freeware and shareware for our example. We are concerned with licensed software for one person.

There are various versions of this story but I will tell the story as it was related to me among the lab aides and students at the community college, where I was later a lab manager. There is a lot of academic discussion about this topic and a lot written but I lived through these times and I want to relay what I feel was the story circulated by word of mouth and what affect it had on the laws governing copying illegal software. This story may not be that accurate but then again is any story in the newspaper or on television ever absolutely 100% accurate? The story verbally relayed to me was that two brothers who had a computer store in Lahore, Pakistan were said to have been tired of people illegally copying software, resulting in software companies losing money and deciding not to develop further software packages that the brothers would sell in their store and ultimately make a commission on. This annoyed brothers and they decided to teach the general public a lesson. The brothers, allegedly, put a virus in a Lotus 1-2-3 executable file that triggered some install files when loaded to a host machine if it had been illegally copied, distributed, and installed.

Shinder and Tittel mention the three types of common viruses as boot sector viruses, application or program viruses, and macro viruses [3]. The boot sector virus can be passed from a diskette when it is accessed. Then the virus embeds itself in the master boot record often in sector zero. Then each time the system is booted, the virus gets loaded into the system. Some viruses today have a feature built in to not allow various anti-virus software programs to run to remove them. It seems as if there is an arms race between the virus writers and the ant-virus software makers.

The second type of virus is the program virus. This virus loads onto the host machine when the application is run. The virus could possibly be embedded in the executable file, but more than likely would be linked to files that install during the installation process and then the virus would be either infected in the master boot record or perhaps only run when the application is run. A lot depends on how the virus writer wishes to demonstrate his level of discomfort on the victim.

The third type of virus is the macro virus. Many people have no idea what a macro is so I will explain the macro first before I discuss its transmission in a virus. It is a little applet that runs and allows a person to perform a complex task by automating it. The macro is triggered by selecting a chord, meaning two keys pushed together, such as Control-M, to do some batch task such as load a template with the correct formats and prepare the machine and printer to print mailing labels. I used to like macros when they were first available in software packages like PFS Write because they allowed senior citizen volunteer employees with some motor impairment the ability to perform commonly used tasks by pushing two buttons together to do a set of steps to perform a task. You can record a macro as you do any common set of tasks, and then stop recording, and give it a chord such as "Control W."

I thought macros were software developers gift to the elderly too because people with cognitive impairment or new to computers were not worried how to accomplish all the individual steps (mechanics) of the work, but could focus on the work itself. The use of macros meant less calls to me when I ran the help desk as a government employee. Some senior citizen volunteer workers would use macros extensively but then they would find the macro would get corrupted and they forgot how to do the original steps to do the task such as printing mailing labels. I then stopped using macros and taught people how to do the work as a series of logical steps. However; many people still use macros and these macros are included with the document when people email them to you. Sometimes when you get an email with a document it will ask you to enable macros. I always answer no because there has never been an occasion where someone sent me a function list of macros and how they are used along with an emailed document attached.

People who write viruses can make them into a macro or disguise them as a macro. That is why many companies have a policy that their employees should never enable macros that accompany a document attached to an email. Now you can understand and appreciate why policy and education with regard to daily operating procedures are just as important as the technical side of security.

12.1.1 – Stopping the Spread of Viruses

We know that we should not enable macros from documents that are emailed to us, especially if they are from people we do not know. This is one strategy to reduce the viruses we all get, but what about all the other viruses that can be downloaded and enabled surreptitiously when you visit certain websites? The answer is to make sure you run an antivirus program that scans attachments on any email you receive. You should also run a full scan on your hard drive at boot-up time.

Some government workers I know have asked to know about all the viruses that come about daily. An old version of an antivirus software program will not check for new viruses unless the software has been manually or automatically updated. I feel that most people will forget to manually check for updates, so setting it to automatic is better. Automatic updates will also be done faster because each time you connect to the Internet, your antivirus software will check its signatures with the latest ones available and automatically update if necessary.

Some viruses have some eccentricities to them. In the mid 1990s I was a lab manager at a community college and we were warned about a Michael Angelo virus that only appears to be active on March 6 each year. I instructed my lab workers on March 5 to set the date ahead to the March 7 in the bios of each machine. It was the simple solution until I could get an update with the proper anti-virus signatures. Only a few machines in the lab had Internet connectivity back then, and downloading software was slow and unreliable.

12.2 – The Logic Bomb Crime

There was an employee who was really disgruntled with his engineering company, Omega Engineering, and placed what was known as a logic bomb in his company. The program checked the ex-employer's system clock and went off on a certain date. It caused about ten million dollars in damage and the man was sentenced to forty one months in prison because of his evil deed [3]. Such actions can cause economic harm to any company by diverting funds from new research and development projects or funds originally destined to give better health care coverage to hard working and conscientious employees.

12.3 – Things in Bad Taste

Retired General Claudia Kennedy said in her book that when she went to a school during her military career, the instructors threw in a slide of a young nude woman to wake up the male members of a class [4]. I attended a conference some years ago where a professor once said, "Oops wrong slide", and it had a quick glimpse of a young woman in a French maid outfit. The men grinned but the women found it promoted a culture of sexism which still exists in some places in America. It is best to not add slides with anything that might offend gender or ethnicity. At the same conference, the same professor showed a presentation with a virtual classroom and various animations. One of the distractions was an avatar of a women teacher with a skirt that was too high and the clothes too tight. One woman stood up and angrily said that avatar of a woman was obviously created by a man. It is best to have people review your work before presenting it to avoid sexism and making certain elements of the crowd uptight.

12.4 – Hacking Tools and Mail Bombs

Many colleagues at other universities tell me that whenever you talk about hacking tools or computer warfare tools, the traditional college age student wakes up in class. The sudden interest in questionable topics suggests there is an unnatural interested in doing forbidden things or things with a taboo. Hacking tools are basically tools that allow you to break and enter a website or an IP address. A simple search on the Internet for hacker tools will produce thousands of links. If you click on some of these links, you will find that something more than the web page gets loaded on your machine and it may not work properly or settings suddenly change to allow less security. Be warned!

When it comes to seeing a good presentation on hacking tools, there is a fellow named David Rhoades who is a security professional who has a presentation called, "Hacking for the Masses" that discusses web based hacking tools and their user friendliness. Shinder and Tittel paraphrase Rhoades in their book and suggest the tools are so easy and user friendly to use that your grandmother could bring down a few servers with no problem. But, again, don't try this at home – the consequences may be more than you bargained for and of course are illegal.

There is a program called Quickfire32 that is readily available on the Internet and is reported there to be extremely easy to use and has a nice Windows interface. If You type in an email address and hit Send, the recipient gets 32,000 emails (which of course is illegal and please do not do it). This is a mail bomb and will fill someone's email box up with junk so they cannot even get anymore email until the account is reset and the emails are cleared. It can also cause the mail server at the recipient's email address to shut down because it is getting more mail then it can handle. Mail bombs can cross international borders. They are illegal. Do not try this. I only mention these tools so you know they exist and can plan to defend against them in any security plans you may develop.

12.5 – The Concept of Triangles and the Crime Triangle

Recently there has been an interest in describing triangles and we see emergency management, fire science, and other disciplines describing things in terms of triangles. The triangle is used in many distance learning classes because it is effective and easy to visualize. We see in the fire triangle that one leg is fuel, the other leg is fire, and the third leg is oxygen. If one of the legs is missing, you do not have a fire and you do not have a triangle. People learning fire-science realize this and think about extinguishing fires in terms of the triangle. If water was blasted in by hose to tackle an electrical fire in a room full of computers, the result would be total ruin; so they rule that out. However; the water would smother the fire and eliminate one leg of the triangle. Then the fire chief thinks if it is possible to remove the fuel. There is no valve to turn off and it will stop. Then perhaps the fire chief says we can remove the oxygen and sees there is a Halon gas system for the room. They shut all doors and windows and let the Halon gas loose. The fire is often out in fifty seconds without oxygen.

The crime triangle consists of opportunity, means, and motive as in figure 12.1. Shinder and Tittel discuss the crime triangle on page 354 of their text which I highly recommend because in my opinion it is so easy to read. They say you cannot remove motive. People have all kinds of motives from greed to curiosity. Some people will even want to break in because they see it as a challenge. We know that sometimes breaking in can be politically inspired as we see with many of the Cyber war actions between Palestinians and Israelis in the Middle East. Sometimes one of those parties will deface the website of their opponent which can mean altering a picture to something unflattering or obscene. One should never go in a computer without proper authorization.

It is also impossible to stop the means. Tools like the ones David Rhoades speaks of are way too circulated and even if they are illegal in some countries they would not be illegal in every country and people would get them from there or perhaps in some kind underground black market. Some tools like NMAP are used for vulnerability assessment but can be used by hackers for nefarious purposes too. You cannot stop the spread of such tools when many have legitimate purposes.

The only thing you can even hope to stop is the means or vulnerability by which they can get into your machine. Many people who do hacking exploit the vulnerabilities of Windows as well as the Windows browser known as Internet Explorer. Many of the Windows users have gotten tired of the constant buying of firewalls, anti-spyware programs, downloading patches, and installing security packs and have switched to Linux based machines. Linux is an operating system that is pretty secure and hackers do not bother much with it.

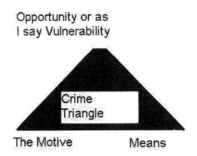

Figure 12.1 – The Crime Triangle Described by Shinder and Tittel

12.6 – Violent Cybercrime

Suppose there is a fellow named Billy and he is part of an office of people that is getting downsized. Billy's boss retains his girlfriend who works in the office and some of the guys who party with the boss after work but Billy gets made redundant or fired as we say in America. Billy is really angry with his boss for firing him. Billy knows his IP address and watches his every move with a variety of tools. That is Cyberstalking and is a violent crime. If Billy uses an anonymous email re-mailer and sends an email to his boss saying he will get him after work at the bar one evening, it is "assault by threat." If Billy uses those simple tools that David Rhoades speaks about to "bring down a few servers," to reduce company profits and get even with the company, then that is Cyber-terrorism. The police give high priority to violent crime. Be warned!

12.7 – Becoming a Cyber-Investigator

In the early 2000s, we have seen a lot of jobs being off-shored, outsourced, or just disappearing as the nature of work changes. We see in the popular media and from the complaining of personal friends that more and more people are out of work and needing another career. The popular media reports more people are getting scammed on the Internet and Cyber-crime is on the rise. The rise of Cybercrime may lead you to consider a career in Cyber-investigation due to the prevalence of crime.

Let me relay a story about a man who was losing his job and needed retraining. There was a fellow who was a student at the university I once worked for who told me after class one day, he was out of work because of downsizing. He said he worked in a military avionics company and his company gave him six months pay and enough money to complete his education. That was generous. He was looking for a new career.

Suppose he wanted to become a Cyber-investigator and would take my advice. I could give him many avenues of advice for success but will tell you one of them now. I would tell him to take classes at FDU such as Introduction to Network Security, Computer Security Administration, Forensic Expert, and Issues in Cybercrime. Then at the university, he could get a nice certificate in Computer Forensics and Security Administration. I would also advice him to take a 2 day class such as the Paraben PDA Seizure and Examination Class so he has a specialty that was marketable such as being able to seize and examine blackberry units. I only mention this because I am aware of these course programs. There are many good course programs out there for learning. I would also ask him to take a couple summer classes in accounting and a class in technical writing. Lastly I would suggest he take a private investigation class and get a certificate. Then he could intern with a private detective agency. If they liked him, they would hire him and he could work under their license doing computer investigations and other investigative work to earn a living.

Then they might send him to a Cyberfraud investigator class. Depending on his previous work experience, his ability to write reports, his patience and persistence, his ability to investigate accounting audit trails on the computer, and finally present evidence to a jury. He might become a very esteemed Cyber-fraud investigator.

After working on so many cases under someone else's license, he may take some tests, fill out some papers and get approved by the State Police to become a private investigator. After so many years he may obtain a private investigator's agency license and start his own agency and hire a lot of ex-police.

The last thing I want you to think about is that you should not get your ideas about being a private investigator from watching television. There is a show called Magnum P.I. where Tom Selleck drives this red Ferrari that makes him stand out like a sore thumb. Investigators should be low key and blend in. Another set of movies about private investigators that only serve as a source of good entertainment is the Tony Roma movies with Frank Sinatra. You should get your ideas from talking to real police detectives, real private investigators, and you can get an internship with a real private investigation firm even if it does not pay anything. There is no method of learning an industry like being in it. An internship will let you determine what parts of the business are good for you as far as your likes and dislikes and you can determine what pays well and what does not. My opinion for whatever its worth is that forensic accounting and Cyber investigator skills may make you a nice living as you change jobs working for bigger and bigger agencies, and acquire more and more skills.

REFERENCES

1. Titel, E., Shinder, D., (2002) "Scene of the Cybercrime Computer Forensics Handbook", Syngress Books, ISBN 1-931836-65-5, Page 27
2. URL Visited August 4,2005, http://www.totse.com/en/viruses/virus_information/allvirus.htm
3. Titel and Shinder, Page 337-338
4. Kennedy, C., (2001),"Generally Speaking", Abridged version for books on tape, Time Warner Audio Books, ISBN 1-58621-175-7

Chapter 13 –
Removing Unwanted Processes, Enforcing Policy

13.0 – Introduction

There are programs that run on your computer known as processes. If you hit the Control, Alternate, and Delete buttons at the same time you will see the taskmgr.exe process running as in figure 13.1 and it displays a list of processes running on your system. Some processes belong to the user, (*see below:* User Name: "eamon"), who is the person logged on to the system. Some processes such as taskmgr.exe belong to the operating system. The processes take a certain amount of memory, known as RAM, to run. The RealPlay.exe process allows me to watch instructional videos for distance learning. It is running as a background process and I only need to click on its icon at the bottom of the screen and bring it to the foreground and load a video to watch. It takes up over two Megabytes of memory.

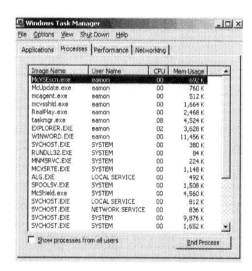

Figure 13.1 – Processes Running on Windows XP Home Edition

Sometimes if you visit certain websites of private individuals who are hacktivists for example, you may notice a popup window showing the downloading of a series of items such as the webpage and some other files. Sometimes files get downloaded and cause processes to run on your system without your consent. You should check the task manager to see the processes running as in figure 13.1 and if one of the processes looks like it is taking a lot of memory, has an odd name, or is one that you do not recognize, then type its name into the google search engine. You maybe amazed to learn that some processors are data mining processes that report your web browsing habits to advertisers. I had one of these data mining processes on my computer some years back that looked at some car dealership sites I viewed. I soon had some pop up windows that appeared telling me about instant credit for car loans and car accessories.

A law enforcement officer had shown a group of information security students a program called "Hijack This." The program showed all the processes running on a system and allowed you to easily select one to investigate what it did as well as how to terminate the process. The task manager in Windows lets you select processes and click on a button labeled "End Process" as in figure 13.1. However; I have had processes from viruses running that could not be terminated with the task manager. You would need to purchase a program like "Hijack This", install it on your computer, then terminate the process; proving that there is a way to do.

Some malicious programs spawn child processes that will quickly spawn children processes at exponential rates until the random access memory (RAM) in the computer is completely filled. Then the computer appears to stop working. Other processes could be known as keystroke loggers and either store or show a remote hacker, in real time, every key that you hit: which can expose secure websites, usernames, passwords, and credit card numbers. You may wish to run Adaware 6.0 to show you any spyware, keyloggers, data miners, and cookies which are now on your machine. Adaware can be seen in figure 13.2. One thing about Adaware is that it needs to be updated quite often, so that it knows about the latest types of programs that could be available to people who put things on your machines.

Running Adaware 6.0 should be part of your weekly routine to check for harmful or unwanted programs and eliminate them. You should also backup your documents once a week and use an uninterruptible power supply to keep your desktop from being disrupted from brief power outages. In the New York City, New Jersey area, there are often times in the summer where they switch generators or there is a brief few seconds of no power due to the number of people turning on their air conditioners and straining the electric power service. The brief interruptions of power are hard resets for your computers. That means it was not brought down and backup properly. This sudden reset causes a process to run that informs me that the file system may have been affected and there will be a check for disk consistency. I am sure that such hard resets have some negative effect on the system. Since I have been using a UPS, I have found that these hard resets have stopped in my home office where I like to write. It is best to look at a few models of UPS systems on the web and call up a manufacturer and get the correct size one that will handle all the peripherals you need to connect to it.

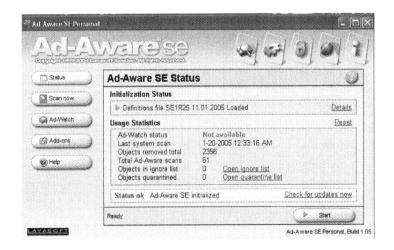

Figure 13.2 – Adaware Version 6.0

13.1 – Proactive Approach to Keep Away Unwanted Processes From Floppy Disks

There was a program in 2004 through the National Science Foundation that made money available for colleges and universities in the United States to help create an Information Assurance curriculum. Part of the key to getting funding was to incorporate computer security, information security, and network security concepts and practices into the curriculum. The participating school also had to demonstrate it was practicing information security and not just preaching it. There are many processes (virus') that are spread from one computer to another via floppy disks.

One of the recommendations was to stop using floppy disks on the system and to use CDs. The policy of not using floppy disks can be enforced by two means. The first to physically disable the drive by disconnecting the ribbon to the floppy drive inside the machine and hopefully the machine has a lock and key. The second way is to go into the operating system in Windows XP and through the control panel, system, device manager, and find the floppy drive. Then right click on the floppy drive and there will be an option to disable the drive as in figure 13.3. You will be prompted, "Do you really want to disable the drive and it tells you it won't work." Then you can disable the drive. In a school environment, you need to make sure only the administrator account can disable the drive because students will re-enable it and disregard the lab's policies.

Figure 13.3 – Disabling a Drive to Enforce Policy

Shinder and Tittel discuss that some people who use computers feel they are above or beyond the law [1]. I have personally witnessed such phenomena as a lab manager and as an instructor throughout my educational and professional career. I have also observed many lab managers who have explained why policies exist, posted the policies, made them available on the web, and even had people sign them after swearing that they have read and understood the policy. However, people often refuse to follow policy no matter what you do because of arrogance on their part. The only way to enforce policy is to have an administrator account and student accounts in a school that follow a template with limited use of the operating system. Student accounts should have the control panel disabled because they can reconfigure hardware, software, and give themselves privilege beyond their authority. In a corporate environment, the regular employee should have a limited account with the same privileges that other employees of his occupation or workgroup have in the organization have.

If a person is a clerk, one can use a clerk template that allows privileges to accounts a clerk would need and forms and printers a clerk would need to use. That account needs to be configured with limited access to drives, folders, files, and printers relevant to that person's occupation and department. The employee or student cannot be relied upon to follow any policy which often restricts where they are allowed to go. Both the student and employee need to have an account that is tailored to their position in the company or school. Sometimes policies that protect the good of everyone such as not using floppy drives are made so that harmful processes are not introduced into the workplace or learning environment. However; it should only be through the administrator's account policy that such disabling is enforced. Policies need to be enforced in a fair manner among everyone.

REFERENCES

1. Titel, E., Shinder, D., (2002) "Scene of the Cybercrime Computer Forensics Handbook", Syngress Books, ISBN 1-931836-65-5, Page 111-112

Chapter 14 –
Introduction to Computer Forensics

14.0 Introduction – Whenever you encounter a term such as computer forensics, a good definition is needed. Many traditional age college students will say," Who cares about a definition?" How can anyone understand the concept of computer forensics and what it encompasses without a good working definition? The other problem that you may encounter is that sometimes people in industry, academia, and occasionally law enforcement will use the term computer forensics interchangeably with computer security and though some topics may overlap, the two terms and what they encompass are very different. One of my previous bosses in private industry believed in the escalator ride rule for expressing ideas for new policies, products, and definitions. If I could not explain my idea for a new product, policy, or a definition by the time we finished the escalator ride, it was either a bad idea, a bad definition, or I was not sufficiently prepared to discuss my subject. When the boss reached the top of the escalator, he would invite me to the office to tell him more if my concise idea on the escalator ride had captured his interest.

The escalator rule is also very useful because one day you may be an expert witness in a computer forensics case and will have to qualify as an expert by the process called "Voir Dire" that we discussed in a previous chapter. One of the first things that may happen in the "Voir Dire" process is that the opposing attorney will ask you the definition of computer forensics. If you hesitate, falter, and use words such as um, the weight of your testimony will certainly be reduced and will negatively impact the case perhaps allowing someone to go free or get a reduced sentence. I would suggest you go back and check the references for each chapter because it is my opinion there are some useful books that explain courtroom decorum and its effect on a case.

I am quite sure any boss who uses the escalator rule would also like the definition presented by the combined efforts of authors Bill Nelson, Amelia Phillips, Frank Enfinger, and Chris Steuart in their textbook called, "Guide to Computer Forensics and Investigations" They define computer forensics in their glossary as "applying scientific methods to retrieve data and/or information from digital evidence. [1]" I felt the definition might be considered by some to be incomplete because I thought someone might ask what digital evidence is. That text did not have a definition of digital evidence in their glossary.

Eoghan Casey has a book on digital evidence and computer crime that presents a definition you might find more enlightening. Casey says, "the term digital evidence encompasses any and all digital data that can establish a crime has been committed or can provide a link between a crime and its victim or a crime and its perpetrator" [2]. John Vacca, a former policeman, offers a useful addition to the definition. Vacca says, "computer forensics involves the preservation, identification, extraction, and documentation of computer evidence stored as data or magnetically encoded information"[3]. Vacca's definition might be the most enlightening description of computer forensics to someone who knows nothing about it.

It is noteworthy that all evidence must be collected legally, which means within the policies of a corporation by an incident response team, or by a sworn law enforcement officer following the laws of the land where he or she has jurisdiction. You might be getting the idea that there are two types of computer forensic investigations. The first is a policy violation in a corporation that that turns into a criminal case where police, FBI, Scotland Yard or Interpol might be brought in. The other type of case is the criminal case that starts in the community.

14.1 – Working for a Private Investigator

You may decide to become a private investigator and work for a private investigation agency that does computer investigations for private individuals. You may work under someone else's license until you get your license. I can give you an example of a case you might work on. Suppose a woman calls the private investigation agency (PIA) and suspects her husband of infidelity and hires the PIA to investigate. The agency might collect $150 per hour and perhaps you might get half depending on the arrangement you have with the agency. You would most likely first visit and collect her name, her husband's name, make sure they were who they say they were, and see the marriage license. Then you would collect any other facts pertaining to the case, assign a case number, and create a folder. You would need to make sure you had proper permission to search their computer. In a relationship of two married people where common property such as a computer is held, it is my lay opinion that the wife can give consent to search the entire machine if the husband had no special arrangements such as encryption which he thought would give him an expectation of privacy. However; since I am not a lawyer and only trying to teach broad concepts; it is best if you get a professional opinion on that. Then once you have all the facts and legal permissions, you can proceed.

I described all of that because the woman who called could have been a house sitter and not the owner of the computer. This would have caused great legal trouble for everyone. Once everything is lawful, then perhaps the private investigator runs a program such as WinHex from a thumb drive he or she plugs in the USB port. Perhaps the investigator then runs on a search of all used and unused space on the drive for a key phrase such as "meet you after work." This could reveal a temporary file with the last name .tmp which included remnants of chat room conversation with sentences such as, "don't worry my wife will think you are one of my clients from the modeling agency." Then that cluster, a multiple of 512 bytes, can be searched for more digital evidence to confirm or deny her suspicions.

The private investigator should also take some classes in psychology and criminal justice to learn more about human behavior. The private investigator may then ask questions during the interview that would give a better idea of the husband's behavior and lead to key words to look for in the search. Dee Moody, a licensed polygraph examiner, also suggests looking for non verbal clues such as changes in facial expression, tone of voice, body postures, and physical gestures. Interviewing a person is an art and you really need to follow seven keys of effective listening which are: listen actively, listen perceptively, listen accurately, listen objectively, listen with empathy, listen patiently and persistently, and listen without getting irritated [4].

Van Norstrand, a coauthor of Moody, and Moody, also reminds you to interview people with another person accompanying you if possible because a partner can witness a statement and a partner can protect you from accusations of improper conduct including sexual harassment, intimidation, or physical abuse [5]. Frank Sinatra plays the character Tony Roma in a 1967 movie and Tony will sometimes intimidate someone he is seeking information from. Television and movies are not the place to learn interviewing techniques. The interviewing techniques should be learned from proper educational material. The interview if done properly, can lead to clues that will save the investigator a lot of time and cut to the chase as they say. There is a question and answer phase, verification and testing phase, and a closing phase. Interviews can also be hostile, neutral, or friendly.

The trained investigator can also ask pertinent questions that the untrained interviewer might find awkward such as "Did your husband suddenly get interested in going to the gym and improving his appearance?" Some law enforcement personnel have told me that such questions can indicate a new romantic interest. I feel questioning is an art and the more one knows about human behavior, the better.

14.2 – Checking the Internet History

Suppose you are working on an alleged marital infidelity case mentioned above and found out through examining the conversation in the temp file that it was from a chat room conversation, and that the husband had started a new gym membership. Perhaps the wife noticed the husband was working later more often and had a new interest in his appearance. You, the investigator, can also check the Internet History File by going into Microsoft Windows Explorer and finding the Internet History File and see the last twenty URLS he looked at. Perhaps the last 20 sites have to do with Internet dating sites for singles. One could say perhaps they all resulted from popup window ads. Then one can go to the DOS prompt, type REGEDIT and get to the registry. In the registry, there is a section that says "Typed in URLS." This can refute a claim that they were all from pop up ads because they were typed in. The way to get to the "Typed in URLS" is by means of a long path. First start with HKEY_CURRENT_USER, then select SOFTWARE, then INTERNET EXPLORER, then TYPED URLs as in Figure 14.1

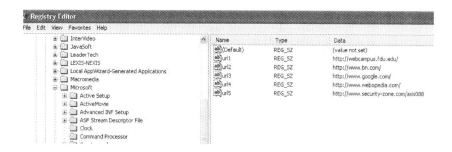

Figure 14.1 – Typed URLS for the Current User of Internet Explorer

Then the licensed private investigator or a person working under his license in lawful circumstances may follow the husband's car, take pictures from a public place, examine digital evidence, and ultimately create a report. The report is given to the client and the client pays for the report. Pictures, interviews, and digital evidence may all support a common set of behaviors and be used by the client to confirm or deny a suspicion. The private investigator is finished with that case unless it goes to a divorce court and the private investigator is asked to testify.

14.3 – Other Tools for Collecting Evidence

The private investigator (PI) could have asked the woman in the previous investigation for permission to connect a keycatcher to the back of the unit between the unit and the keyboard cable. There are strict laws on using the keycatcher and it is necessary for the private investigation agency to make sure the use complies with local laws. The keycatcher can allow replay of everything typed in at the computer since it was installed. Then later, the PI would start up MS-Word, hit a couple keys and everything typed in since the keycatcher was installed would be on the screen. The keycatcher often holds the last 32 kilobytes of information typed. It is really important to follow the law for digital evidence search and seizure or the investigator and person hiring the PI could be in big trouble.

Figure 14.2 – The Blackberry

14.4 – The Blackberry and Handheld Devices

It is very important to understand that there is a convergence of technologies and it is getting more difficult to say what is a cell phone, a computer, or some type of hybrid combination thereof. I will now direct your attention to the Blackberry which has the properties of a cell phone as well as those of a computer. The Blackberry shown in figure 14.2 allows email to be composed, sent and received with certain size text attachments. A person in the drug trade for example could send emails to another person about buying, selling, or trading drugs for stolen merchandise. There is also a calendar which can mark events and even be used with an alarm. There is an address book with ample room for contacts. Each contact can store email addresses, phone numbers, fax numbers, and various other home and work point of contact (POC) data. There is also a call log showing all incoming and outgoing phone messages. There is also Internet connectivity that allows you to search text based documents. I personally consider my Blackberry useful and nicely constructed and it can easily last up to 48 hours without recharging. There are many other handheld devices other than the Blackberry that would be just as useful.

14.45 – A Simulated Example Simple Case Involving a Blackberry
Let's suppose my friend's brother Eddy Jr. said, "Quit bothering me at odd hours with your blackberry and hanging up after an extended period of time!" I would say I was not doing that and I could easily check my phone log on the Blackberry. I could also connect a cable on the side of the Blackberry and connect the other end into my USB port. I could then run my software from the Paraben Corporation that allows me to connect to the Blackberry which uses the RIM operating system. Once connectivity is established, there is an icon I can click and acquire the image of all the memory in the machine. That includes all used and unused sections. In a matter of less than one minute I would have the entire memory contents on my laptop. Then I can use the emulator available in Paraben to simulate a Blackberry Environment, I could then see everything that the Blackberry user would see without depriving someone the use of the Blackberry. I would not alter the original data on the Blackberry. I could search the image of the drive for "Eddy Jr" or his number and see if there were any clues to why he may suspect I called him from my machine.

I've found out from personal experience that if the Blackberry is not in a case and the keyboard is not locked, it can accidentally be calling people and I would not be aware of it. If Eddy Jr. had his answering machine on, I could inadvertently call him and be transmitting to his answering machine until I move in a way that hits buttons and disconnects the call or until Eddy Jr.'s answering machine is full and disconnects the call. Strange things happen – be warned!

Just imagine that the following technical scenario occurs in a real life situation on the street: suppose that a police detective had called a known drug dealer to ask about a known problem on the street and then they talk and terminate the call. Later in the day, the dealer has his Blackberry in his pocket, moves around, it calls up the last contact who was the policeman, and a drug buy winds up being recorded on the policeman's answering machine. The caller ID log would indicate the identity of the caller. It would be interesting to examine the legal aspects of using the digital evidence to prosecute an illegal drug sale when the dealer's sole defense was that the Blackberry inadvertently called the policeman. Computer forensics can involve technical and legal issues. It is this intersection of the law and technology that may make it an exciting career for you.

Eamon P. Doherty Ph.D.

REFERENCES

1. Nelson, B., Phillips, A., Enfinger, F., Steuart, C., (2004), "Guide to Computer Forensics and Investigations", Published by Thompson Course Technology, ISBN 0-619-13120-9, Page 651
2. Casey, E., (2001), "Digital Evidence and Computer Crime", Published by Academic Press, London, England, Page 1, ISBN 0-12-162885-X
3. Vacca, J., (2002),"Computer Forensics, Computer Crime Scene Investigation", Published by Charles River Media, Hingham, MA, ISBN 158450-018-2
4. Van Nostrand, G., Moody, D., (1996), "Truth-Finding Methods: Interview and Interrogation Techniques", Thompson Education Direct, Pages 4-7
5. Van Nostrand and Moody, " ", Page 13

Chapter 15 –
Some Basic Legal Principles for Computer Forensics People

15.0 – Introduction

A computer science person generally cannot just say s/he knows something about computers and automatically be a successful computer forensics professional because s/he is most likely lacking the education principles regarding the collection and examination of digital evidence. A policeman too cannot generally declare say s/he knows something about search and seizure and the law and be a successful computer forensics professional without of all the educational principles needed in computer science. This chapter will also discuss some of the cultural issues generally perceived to exist between computer scientist types and policeman who must now work together in computer investigations. This cooperation between computer scientist/ programmer types and law enforcement has evolved as a result of the plethora of computing equipment and operating systems that now exist and it is nearly impossible for small private and public organizations to have experts on hand for all the devices available to the general public. Sometimes new and unique partnerships are emerging across government, education, and the private sector to address gaps in security or because of the new funding opportunities promoted by Homeland Security.

15.0.1 – Serving Your Country with Your Knowledge of Security and/or Networks

If you are an academic with skills that may be relevant to security, you may volunteer to become a member of a Homeland Security Consortium at both the university and the state level. It is possible for you to meet a lot of people from the military, law enforcement, army civilian scientists, intelligence agencies, and municipal employees. So if you want to learn more about security and make a contribution to the United States, you can volunteer your time and be a part of a Homeland Security Consortium. There are numerous consortiums in various sections of the United States.

Perhaps you do not want to become a member of a consortium and attend meetings. You would like to have a more personal connection for helping support the person on the front lines who keep America safe. If you are a ham radio operator and enjoy combining digital modes of communications and radio equipment to communicate with people, you could join Army Military Amateur Radio Service (MARS). You may use a terminal node controller that is connected to your computer and connected to a radio. That radio can be connected to a directional antenna known as a "Yagi" that can be connected to the chimney. Such a set up is not very expensive and allows you to connect to a wide range of hobbyists in the United States. Many terminal node controllers support various digital formats such as AMTOR, PACTOR, and radio teletype. You could even help Army personnel abroad communicate with loved ones in the US.

As a ham radio operator, in addition to using the digital communication modes, you may also enjoy talking on the radio with other operators and being part of a "net" which is slang for a group of people connected by a wireless network. If your radio supports certain frequencies around above the 80 meter band (3.5 Megahertz) and various VHF frequencies, you may wish to become a United States Navy Military Amateur Radio Service Operator, Navy MARS, and pass messages of health and well being to and from family members of submarine personnel.

15.1 – The Cultural Perception of the Information Technology Professional (ITP)

I have also been a corporate computer consultant, and a member of an exercise facility where I met many people in information technology from large fortune five hundred companies. I have also lived in England where I have obtained my doctorate and spent time at universities in various parts of the United States and Hong Kong. I have experienced a variety of cultures and attitudes and feel qualified to express some perceptions of cultures that I feel are held by many. These are my opinions and do not reflect my place of business or our affiliates.

I was also reading some literature that agreed with my own opinions that I will now express. I found that many information technology professionals have to put in long hours because as we said in a previous chapter, computer technology frequently changes. These long hours of learning and gaining proficiency are often done after work and often mean sitting in front of computer until midnight. This learning and proficiency may be in the form of organized learning in classes or informal learning by reading a manual and experimenting with software. Since no one can be in two places at once this often leads to an absence in civic organizations and participating in town meetings and community as well as social activities. This absence contributes to the perception in the community that the information technology professional is not interested in the community, or a bit of a nerd.

Many information technology professionals reward themselves with new cars and luxury items because they have little time to enjoy the money they earn. New cars and other displays of material wealth when combined with an absence in community activities can create a perception of being preoccupied with wealth. The information technology sector often changes and some professionals have to strategically manage their career by changing jobs and moving location to learn new skills, practice them and stay employable. This often can create a perception that the information technology professional is chasing dollars and has few roots in a community.

Computer science requires innovative thinking to solve new situations and by its nature attracts students who tend to be very creative and "think outside of the box" if I may use that overused cliché. Popular culture in TV and media often portray many computer programmers and scientists as possibly too liberal in their personal politics. I hope I have successfully described part of the information technology industry and how it can be perceived by the community. Now we will examine the public sector.

15.1.1. – The Culture of the Law Enforcement Professional (LEP)

From my own personal contacts with the law enforcement professional (LEP) and from what I have garnered from the newspaper, it is my personal opinion the LEP is usually a highly dedicated individual who often lives in the community s/he serves. S/he is often low paid as compared to other skilled professions in the private sector, and must often work holidays, evenings, night shift, and is generally on call at a moment's notice to protect and serve the community in a time of crisis. The law enforcement professional must maintain a professional demeanor even off duty which is a form of stress the information technology worker does not have to deal with. Some LEPs I have met have expressed an opinion that there are people watching law enforcement people on and off duty who can't wait to point out a fault. This too can create stress.

Once the law enforcement professional has worked seven or eight years in the community, they will have really "invested" in their pension and finding another job and transferring the pension may not be feasible. That probably causes stress. Just by the nature of the jobs, many law enforcement professionals deal with people with problems all day and see crime that the average person could never comprehend. This could shape one's outlook and personal political views.

15.1.2. – When the IT and LEP Work Together
There are times when the law enforcement professional (LEP) and the information technology professional must work together. Sometimes there will be a computer investigation where a criminal uses a really obscure computer and/or operating system in the hope that should they be caught, that there will be nobody in the jurisdiction of the alleged crime sufficiently knowledgeable or experienced enough to investigate it. Perhaps someone used an Amiga 2000 in a theft from a bank and then used an obscure word processing package with a proprietary format to store the records. The regional computer forensics lab (RFCL) police most likely do not have an examiner on staff that is proficient with the Amiga 2000. Therefore the police must seek an expert on the Amiga 2000.

The LEP assigned to an investigation with an Amiga 2000 for example can check special interest clubs, expert hobbyist groups posted on the Internet, or look for information technology workers who once developed such systems professionally. Other professional computer forensics incident response organizations such as First (Forum for Incident Response Teams) have computer forensics / IT experts in over thirty countries and may provide good leads and help if the crime exceeds the jurisdiction of the present investigator's jurisdiction and goes overseas.

It is possible that when computer scientists or IT professionals first work together, there could be some friction between the different personalities and cultures. However, all parties, being professionals, will have many things in common which can cause mutual empathy. They often both work evening shifts, holidays, and in some cases, the overnight shift. This can result in mutual respect and friendship known commonly as "bonding". Let us now consider some more things they have in common. The computer programmers and network professionals are bound by the rules and syntax of the operating system. The LEP is bound by numerous laws and department policies and procedures. This commonality can cause a bonding too. The

IT professionals and LEPs often like TV shows such as CSI that combine forensic science, computers and law enforcement.

15.2 – The Early Phases Leading to Investigation

Suppose a person walks their dog everyday in a neighborhood and the dog gets loose and runs to the front bushes of a home to chase a big groundhog. The dog gets its leash stuck in the bushes. The bushes are underneath a window. The person runs over to free the dog and it is a time consuming process as the dog fidgets and the leash is wrapped around the bushes rather extensively. Suppose the owner of the dog hears a person in the house operating a computer and talking on the cell phone about some unexpected problems that arose while attempting to steal some money from a bank. The person would most likely out of civic duty and curiosity, look in the window and get a glimpse of the computer. S/he would probably then unhook the dog from the leash in order to return home carrying the dog and call the police.

Now we will look at a possible scenario of how the police might handle an investigation so you can conceptualize the mechanics of an investigation. Since I am not a legal expert and cannot give legal advice or tell you exactly how a police investigation will be conducted, I will give you a general idea of what is done and why.

The police would come to the house and interview the person making an allegation. Then the officer would take a statement from the person and a formal complaint would be filed and might go on the chief's blotter [1]. The chief may tell the detective to start an investigation. Perhaps the detective determines the computer in question is an Amiga 2000 for example. Then once a complaint is filed, the officer may make an affidavit in front of a judge who will notarize it and perhaps issue a search warrant. The officer may contact someone from the International Association of Computer Investigative Specialists (IACIS) who most likely recommends a local IT professional known as a "Technical Assistant" (TA), who knows the small personal computer known as the Amiga 2000. If the Amiga 2000 was a large unmovable computer with massive storage capability, the TA, may follow the officer in an a support vehicle on the search and seizure to help collect the relevant files in what is commonly known as a sparse evidence file [2]. Depending on the country and local laws, the officer may do a procedure known as "knock and announce." Then the police will enter and speak to the person. Perhaps the discussion reveals a high probability that a theft occurred. They will then seize all relevant electronic equipment such as drives, answering machines, cables, monitors, computers, and answering machines that could hold messages about calls concerning the crime.

Perhaps the technical advisor (TA) might next go to the computer forensics lab at the small town where investigations are performed and help examine the logs and files for evidence of the crime. Suppose the TA finds evidence of a robbery right away, then the person held for questioning, would be charged with a crime, arrested, and be arraigned in front of a judge and a formal charge would be made for trial.

15.3 – The Fourth Amendment

It appears from perusing various documents that the Fourth Amendment applies to criminal cases not involving customs. The Fourth Amendment protects American People in the United States from unlawful search and seizure [3]. However; suppose I was about to export computers from a company that has trade secrets and the computers were not licensed for export and not certified as "sanitized", then customs could potentially seize them without a search warrant to protect trade secrets. There is some literature on the Internet that says Fourth Amendment does not apply to matters of customs and especially with port security. This is a good thing because international containers can quickly be brought inland and could contain contraband shipments that need immediate attention and there may not be time or sufficient evidence for a proper search warrant. It is best if you discuss this situation with legal counsel to get the exact details.

15.4 – Various Legal Systems within the USA

People from outside the United States often see America as one big monolithic country with a uniform set of laws. They are partially correct in that all the states are governed by federal laws which provide a common code of law. However; states have their own laws and their own state governments. The Civil War, also known as the "War Between the States", was also partially about "States Rights" and the ability to self-govern in addition to the issue of the abolition of slavery. Some municipal policemen have privately expressed a sentiment to me that the laws governing the search and seizure of digital evidence in New Jersey are stricter then what United States Federal law requires. Some people in the community express an opinion on the Internet and editorial columns in the newspapers that these laws passed by the New Jersey Legislature make it more difficult for police in New Jersey to do their job as compared to some states in the west or the south.

Louisiana, a southern state near Alabama, was once a colony of France and its law is influenced partially by Napoleonic Law. The states on the eastern seaboard of the United States were part of the original thirteen colonies of England and have an English influence. A property in Virginia or New Jersey may have a deed that predates the formation of the United States and can be traced to the King of England. Rutgers University in New Jersey was established during the reign of King George III of England. The point is that there are still influences of the former parent country on the thirteen states which were based on English Common Law. The state of Wisconsin uses Tort Law since it was once a French territory [3]. My point is that the United States law is not uniform and one has to be aware of historic differences and how that can influence legislation. It is best if the law enforcement professionals have a working relationship with their county prosecutor's office and the section that deals with Cybercrime. It is also good if local law enforcement have a good working relationship with their local RCFL (Regional Computer Forensics Lab) and the state's Attorney General's expert on Cybercrime to discuss the effect of legislation on the search, seizure, and examination of digital evidence for police in that jurisdiction.

The Department of Justice has what I personally, from my viewpoint as an academic with an interest in computer forensics, consider a great document on their website that has practical examples of computer crime cases and demonstrates the application of law to these cases. Many detectives and computer investigators I have met at both the municipal and county government level have remarked how enlightening the document is. http://www.usdoj.gov/criminal/cybercrime/crimes.html

15.5 – Homeland Security Consortiums

Suppose you are an academic at a university, or a military contract employee in information technology, or a former or an active military commander, or a state government employee in the Office of Information Technology, and you may find yourself becoming part of a Homeland Security Consortium. These are partnerships that bring together university, law enforcement, military, and private sector personnel to examine areas of joint interest such as Cyberspace which is protected partly by an entity known as the National Critical Infrastructure Protection.

Sometimes the schools in a Homeland Security consortium will have expertise in areas such as biometrics and behavioral analysis. Sometimes private industry provides Cyber security experts and can partner with universities to develop new systems to help protect the National Transportation Critical Infrastructure. Perhaps a project of joint development could include a system to identify people in public areas such as an airport. Such identification systems can play a part in locating potential suspects at a particular time if a Cybercrime was perpetrated from a public computer kiosk at the airport for example. Research and development work in the US and the UK using sophisticated digital-video and advanced algorithms, has been on the increase since 9/11.

I have noticed that there is a whole different language and culture involved when dealing with military contractors, military computer science people, and military personnel. The culture may be influenced by numerous federal standards that exist for the military and influence the development and use of security products. You might find that more standards and regulations may limit the highly creative solution finder and promote stricter thinking within the box. The language you hear expressed is different from local law enforcement and academia in that there are often many acronyms used in discussions that represent complex systems and ideas. It is best to keep a notebook of the acronyms and then do a Google search after the meeting to learn more about the acronyms and the systems and ideas they represent. You also need to read the supporting public documents and understand the context of what was discussed at the meeting more fully. It is also worth collecting any literature distributed during such consortium meetings to read about other organizations that meeting members are affiliated with to better understand their viewpoints and identify possible synergies with your organization.

15.6 – Exigency

Suppose you aspire to be a law enforcement officer and a digital evidence examiner. There is a legal principle that is advisable for you to understand if you are going to one day search and seize digital evidence. This complex principal is exigency and comprises of a few parts. I am including one example of my non-legal professional opinion of exigency here because it is not included in many computer forensics books but is worth knowing in my opinion. I am not a lawyer and cannot dispense legal advice and am only giving you some ideas. Please investigate exigency on your own with your local police for an exact definition. Exigency has to do with the urgency of a situation.

Suppose there is a missing person named Billy and his roommate knew his last activity using a computer was to chat with a young lady in Moldavia on a dating site. The policeman ask Billy's roommate about his whereabouts and the roommate mentions about the chat line and dating site and says he is never late and always tells people when he will be away. Billy's computer is in the living room and any reasonable person would think the computer would hold clues to Billy's whereabouts. Since there is a degree of urgency to ensure Billy is not in any danger, it is my lay opinion based on the definition of exigency presented, that the policeman could immediately examine the computer without a warrant and Billy's permission but you should check with legal counsel to make sure since I cannot give legal advice or legal opinions.

15.7 – Liability for Investigators
You may have read the last section on exigency and are now thinking, "I could make a wrong decision to a course of action in an investigation and get sued, or perhaps worse, I could worry about my liability and not take a course of action necessary to save a life!" It is my opinion that if you are like most people, you probably worry a lot about liability and wish you had a workshop to help you understand liability so you could make better decisions." I am sure you want to protect National Security to the fullest, bring criminals and policy offenders to justice, but at the same time you worry about violating legal principles, especially privacy. Professional security organizations such as ASIS International offer workshops such as "Liability for Investigators" for example in their 2005 Professional Development Series. You will be better prepared to make important decisions after taking such a course.

15.8 – Certifications
When you look for classes such as "Liability for Investigators", you may wish to look for teachers who also have initials such as CPP and J.D. after their name. The initials J.D. stand for Doctor of Jurisprudence. That means that they successfully completed a course of study in the legal profession. CPP is an acronym meaning, "Certified Protection Professional." This is a much sought after certification in the security world and is recognized world wide.

Suppose you select a class on liability only because you saw it while surfing the Internet. You need to be careful because there are many people without any letters after their names that are only self-proclaimed experts. They may appear to know something but their material may not be up to date or accurate. It is always best to look at the credentials and check to see if those credentials are affiliated and recognized widely in that discipline.

15.8.1 – System Security Certified Practitioner – SSCP
I have been told by various security professionals that the SSCP exam takes approximately 3.5 hours to complete if you are sufficiently prepared. From discussions in my circles of academic and with my private industry contacts, I perceive it is a respected certification and

the test can be taken in person at various locations around the United States, Europe, and the Middle East on a regular basis. If you pass, you are permitted to put the acronym "SSCP" after your name. The last time I checked, the test was in the neighborhood of US$300. The test covers seven domains which nearly everyone in all the books I read on network security acknowledges as important. Each one of the domains is an area of interest such as malware, or malicious software. The domains you must study are malware, data communications, cryptology, response and recovery, auditing and monitoring, administration, and access control. The CISSP certification is the next certification in this series and is also the highest in that series.

Another thing you must check, if you wish to attain SSCP certification, is that you actually have some years of experience in some aspects of network security. It is not merely studying for a test, passing it, and that is it. It is best to check the requirements before taking the test and have some type of proof such as letters, pay stubs and job descriptions, or perhaps a civil service certification. You should also have photo identification with you when taking the test. A passport is a strong credential that is not easily forged and one that is universally accepted. I would also recommend that whether it is your passport or drivers license, the picture should be updated if you have changed a lot. Perhaps you lost a great deal of weight or no longer wear a full beard and people who examine the picture may have doubts about your identity.

I am almost certain that the insurance company that insures your business would be delighted if you ran classes for your employees on information assurance topics such as social engineering, malware, access control, auditing security logs, recovery principles such as backing up data, basic fire safety, and limiting access control. Some insurance companies may give you a small break on your monthly premium if the class is of real substance, practical, and taught by a accredited professional. Many American insurance companies who insure automobiles will give a lower yearly premium to drivers who have taken a safety class. A security or safety class demonstrates some level of recognition to the importance of acting responsibly and with some degree of caution. Employees who have an understanding of network and information security are more likely to act in a manner promoting network security than employees with no concept of security thereby reducing accidents and payouts. This is a new area called Compliance which is fast becoming a recognized way of taking the onus off employers and putting it firmly in the hands of employees, where a need for professional, dedicated work ethics are the norm. In the above example, a reduction in the insurance premium has merit and is not just a nice gesture from the insurance company.

15.8.2. – Security+ Certification
You can become certified in Red Hat Linux which is useful as long as the person you work for uses Red Hat Linux in the workplace. However; if you get a new administration in the organization, it is possible that the person is a "Microsoft Man", so to speak and switches the platform. Then your certification's relevance is diminished in that company because that platform is no longer used. That is why people I know who have obtained security certifications often prefer the SSCP, CISSP, and Security+ certifications which are vendor neutral. People with a vendor neutral platform security certification are probably more willing

to switch platforms if their knowledge and certifications are portable. Let me tell a story to illustrate my point.

I heard this story from a computer professional whose organization had a group who liked the mainframe and ISDN lines while others favored local area networks, client servers, and virtual private networks. The second group said that virtual private networks (VPN) and the Internet was the way to connect remote sites to the central office in order to reduce costs. The customers realized this too and both the customer and leadership of the second group wanted to get rid of private ISDN lines. The customers and second group's leadership also wanted to get away from mainframes and dumb terminals and adopt local area networks, routers, and have a client server relationship to the headquarters. However, there was one man approaching retirement in the first group who had his career invested in the mainframe and would not budge. His security knowledge was exclusively mainframe orientated. The politics of technology and what group is empowered can significantly affect the equipment you choose, the way you connect computers, and the policies your organization adopts.

Security+ Certification is from CompTIA and many people have told me they like the text called, "Security+ Certification for Dummies" written by Lawrence Miller who holds both a CISSP and Security+ certification. The other coauthor Peter Gregory holds a CISSP and wrote another CISSP for Dummies book which is widely read by security professionals. The Security+ for Dummies book has a CD with various tests to allow you to practice so you have a proper idea what you really know and don't have false hopes. A false sense of confidence can lead to disastrous results after you take a day off to take a test, spend the day traveling, taking a test, and paying for the test. It is my opinion you should take a test after you regularly get 90% or better on practice exams because you may also be nervous on the day of the real test and forget things while under pressure.

The Security+ Certification for Dummies guide is said by many to nicely cover the topics you need to know for that exam. Some of the topics are: communications security, infrastructure security, and cryptology, as well as operational and organizational security. I know a few law enforcement professionals who have said they found the certification useful and coupled with other practical training provided by their agency, it gave them an overall understanding that was useful when conducting investigations and for helping explain questions about security related concepts in court.

15.9 – Connectivity and Handheld Computing Devices
I highly recommend you take a class on cell phone examination and a class on PDA seizure and examination sometime, especially if you are planning, or are soon to become a private security or law enforcement professional, so that you can better serve tour organization by conducting lawful examinations on many of the latest equipment being used by the public.

REFERENCES

1. Nelson, B., Phillips, A., Enfinger, F., Steuart, C., (2004), "Guide to Computer Forensics and Investigations", Published by Thompson Course Technology, ISBN 0-619-13120-9, Page 12-13
2. Nelson " ", Page 312
3. Whitman, M., Mattord, H., (2005),"Principles of Information Security", Published by Thompson Course Technology, ISBN 0-619-21625-5, Page 77-79

Chapter 16 –
Selecting a Conference and Publishing a Paper

16.0 – Introduction

Sometime in your career, you may be asked by your employer to go to a conference in your chosen field which could be computer forensics or network security. There are many reasons that you may be asked to go to a conference. Perhaps your organization needs to establish itself more in computer forensics and needs to have a presence at a conference and have a quality paper in a proceedings or journal. Your organization may also feel that in order to expand in its chosen field that more contacts are needed and that is done through personal networking among colleagues at a conference. You may also be asked to attend a conference because there are certain continuing education requirements and monies that must be spent on professional career development. Then there are some people that just want to see what is going on in their chosen field and have a little time away at the poolside.

16.1 – Choosing a Conference

This is a difficult matter for most people because you must first decide what you need to achieve at a conference. If you are an average writer for example and need to publish a paper, it would probably not be advisable to write a paper and submit it in a top conference in your field. You might do well to read some journals and periodicals in your field and then jot down some names and websites of conferences. Then you go to those websites and read about the conference. There is usually a spot that discusses acceptance rates. One year a conference called CHI, Computer Human Interaction, advised on its website that it had a 20% acceptance rate. You would only enter a paper if you did outstanding novel research or had something of great importance to say.

The budget and your location are big factors. Your employer may only allow $1200 for an airplane ticket, meals, conference fee, and hotel. The cost factor also affects the location you choose. Location is a big consideration because if it is in Europe and during the summer, the airplane ticket alone could cost US$1200.00; whereas a conference in Las Vegas in the summer when it is hot could be cheap as US$300. A lot depends on your family status. If you have a family, you might choose a conference in your field where there are things for your wife and children to do separately. Then you can combine both purposes. Perhaps a security conference in Orlando, Florida would also allow your family to see Disney Land while you do your conference. There would be some evenings for your family and you to socialize together at the conference with other attendees and their families.

Then you can look at seeing who attends the conference, the keynote speaker, the type of exhibits in your field that will be there, and if there will be commercial vendors where you can try products, talk to manufacturers and learn about new equipment trends in your field. You can also see if there is a poster session you are interested in, and workshops that you can sign up for. I remember signing up at CHI 1999 for a workshop in Contextual Inquiry and Design with the authors of a book on the same subject. I not only learned what the authors did not put in the book but I got to ask questions of Karen Holtzblatt and her coauthor about software development issues pertinent to my project. It was useful when I was building an application for disabled people. I will now show a sample paper that has to do with the topic of information and security documents. The conference was $50 and within commuting distance of home which fell within my budget. The conference also allowed me to network with a wide variety of security professionals.

Paper Document Reconstruction and Other Paper Security Techniques
By
Eamon Doherty Ph.D., Assistant Professor, School of Administrative Science, Fairleigh Dickinson University, Email Address : Doherty@FDU.EDU

Presented at the August 22, 2005 First FDU Homeland Security Conference

Introduction to Securing Paper Documents

Many people work on sensitive documents in industry with **trade secrets** which include processes such as the secret recipe for "The Thomas' English Muffin." However; people will often leave papers on a desk or in an unlocked filing cabinet and it is unfortunate but often cleaning personnel will often be there for hours unsupervised at night for hours. It is generally known in the security industry that many third party cleaning companies hire people for low wages with minimal if any background checking. It is recommended to do a **"clean desk policy"** where everything is taken off the desk and locked in a filing cabinet, safe, or desk at the end of the workday [1]. We can see how the concept of cleaning people easily accessing documents after work hours is played out in popular culture by the 1993 film "The Firm." Tom Cruise's character who is a lawyer has little trouble accessing another company's paper documents in an office after work hours when he dresses up like a cleaning man to gain access.

The Consequences of Losing Paper Documents

Many organizations often create internal documents with the security designation, **"internal use only."** Such documents are not for public consumption and could divulge counter terrorism strategies or results of ongoing investigations if lost as was the worry when FBI agent John O'Neil lost a briefcase of high level paperwork in the 1990s in the Middle East. The briefcase was later recovered and revealed in an investigation that only his fingerprints were on the paper. However; he felt bad and resigned from the "bureau." There is more than one agent in the FBI named John O'Neil. This man went on to take a security job at the World Trade Center and was killed at the 9-11 tragedy [2]. Paper documents thrown out can also be garbage picked by a process known as **dumpster diving** where people climb in the dumpster and pull apart garbage seeking documents with passwords, usernames, accounts, and financial information such as corporate credit card numbers.

Modern Destruction of Institutional Paper Documents

A nursing home employee in New Jersey had privately told me that they mark documents in a box that must be saved for a legal amount of time with a date of destruction. When that date is reached, they call a destruction service that is bonded for a million dollars to remove and destroy the documents. That company has a truck that comes and shreds and later incinerates the documents. One can find such services in your area by performing an Internet search on document destruction and your state's name. Some nursing homes even have secure locked boxes on each wing for papers with any public health care information to be discarded. Then junk mail and other paper documents that have no consequence if discovered are discarded in the regular garbage. This separation of garbage is also used for medical waste and needles, gloves, or anything with bacteria or viruses is placed in a biohazard box for destruction.

Historical Blunders in Destroying Paper
The public's level of consciousness regarding information security for paper documents was raised by the American Embassy takeover in Iran in 1979. In the 70s, paper documents were shredded into strips before discarding as a **countermeasure** so people rummaging through garbage would not see the information. This is a basic form of **information security**. However; putting everything in shredders and making bags of strips is not sufficient as one would think and I will give you an example to support my opinion. In **1979 the takeover of the United States Embassy in Iran** was imminent and so the employees shredded large amounts of potentially sensitive documents in strips which filled up garbage bags. The Iranians took the bags of shredded documents and spread them out in a warehouse and reassembled the documents by hand. You can read about this famous event and other like it on the Dahle Paper Shredders website [3].

Paper Types
Many people think that a bag of shredded paper is all the same but it is not. Paper has various **thicknesses, colors,** and **texture** depending on the **fiber**. Some paper is made of rice while other is a wood pulp product. It is common knowledge that ancient paper in Egypt was made of a reed known as papyrus. We also speak of purchasing 30 weight paper of 27 weight paper. The term weight has to do with the heaviness of the ream and heavier weights are nice for greeting cards and might be considered by some people to be a cardboard. Some paper is glossy while other paper documents may have a lamination or baked on plastic coating to preserve them.

Strip Shredders
There are various types of paper shredders that you can purchase. There is the shredder that cuts everything in strips. It is my opinion that you can take the contents of the basket of a strip shredder and quickly separate the various strips of paper into similar piles. The paper often has different glossiness, texture, and thickness and can often be separated into piles depending on the level of diversity of the paper. The more diverse or heterogeneous the shredded paper documents are, the faster one can separate the strips of paper. A relative of mine was able to separate the strips of an accidentally shredded document and layout the strips, and reassemble it with scotch tape in approximately 15 minutes. This was probably the methods used by the Iranians who reassembled the documents from the embassy. There is a corporation called **"Church Street Technology"** that uses a system to reconstruct documents by taking each strip in a bag of strips and scanning it. The company uses a proprietary algorithm to assemble

the strips much as a human assembles a puzzle. This could be good for police who need to reassemble documents shredded by criminals before a search warrant can be issued.

Cross Cut Shredders

I have a GBC Shredmaster 75X cross cut shredder that cuts a document in cross cut strips. A few strips were over 6 inches but the majority were 1.5 inches long and had a thickness of slightly larger than 1/8 inches wide. Some strips were also ¼ to ½ inch long too. The cross cut shred strips could be easily separated into piles because the documents I shredded were on very different paper. As an experiment, I took two pieces of paper on different types of paper and shredded them. I then separated the paper and reconstructed the one document. Intelligence agencies use the finest cut crosscut shreds for disposing of top secret documents.

I did not measure the seconds but it took me 3 minutes to separate the pile of two documents. It was amazing how easy it was to examine the paper thickness and texture of the 2 pieces of paper and sort the pieces into piles of the two documents. One was an advertisement from junk mail that advertised a food market. The paper was light and thin to keep mailing costs low. The other paper was a standard 8.5 inch by 11 inch black and white photocopy of a newspaper copy. The shredded photocopy made approximately 323 strips. I used the word approximately because there could be still some strips not visible and stuck in the shredding mechanism. It took 11 minutes to assemble the first 12 pieces and I felt it was much like a puzzle. The problem was that some of the larger pieces were curved and would not stay straight and curled up and fell over.

I could easily keep up a rate of 1 minute per piece to find a match and tape it. I would naturally assume that rate would increase as there were less pieces of paper and the complexity deceased. I found it was very easy to find the top of the newspaper where the name and date is. It was also easy to identify all the pieces of a picture and group them. Since there were 323 pieces and we will assume in a worst case scenario that it took 1 minute per slice to assemble, that would mean it would take 5 hours and 38 minutes per document to assemble. The rate of 1 minute per piece would diminish if there were more than one document of similar type and grouping pieces into like documents was not simple.

The one thing that makes it significantly more difficult to assemble a document as opposed to a puzzle is that a puzzle has interlocking edges and you can tell right away if there is a fit. In a puzzle, the flat edges indicate the outside of the puzzle where as in a document each strip is cut perfectly straight and determining the outside of a document is nearly impossible without prior knowledge of the document.

Labor

Suppose you wish to reconstruct the document but are reluctant to contract the pieces out, you could probably have a special policeman such as the type used for parades and town fairs do the work. Suppose your town pays $10 per hour and the special policeman is a novice at document reconstruction and works at the same rate as myself (1 piece per minute). Then it would cost approximately $55.00 per document to reassemble. Let's assume in a best case situation that the special policeman could rebuild 2 documents per day, that is too slow and would cost approximately $110.00 to do. My other concern is that the work may be considered boring by some special policeman and might not wish to do the task though they are getting paid.

I did a google search on document reconstruction and found Church Street Technology. Their frequently asked questions page says the price of the job depends on the condition of the shreds, the amount of shreds to be reconstructed, and the size and shape. Their website says they can also reconstitute other languages than English. That can mean languages such as Chinese that consist of tens of thousands of symbols or a language such as Arabic that goes right to left and has its letters change in the word depending on if they are in the beginning, middle, or end of the word. It is possible to arrange with Church Street Technology for a person to testify as an expert witness in the mechanics of documentation reconstruction techniques. The expert would probably give better credibility to the evidence by the court than untrained "special" mentioned above. Their telephone number is 713-877-8832.

Flash Paper and Water Soluble Paper and Illegal Betting
The United States Government estimates that more than $200 million dollars is spent on illegal gambling. It is also very difficult to catch the criminals in their headquarters, also known as "the wire room", for these operations because many "bookies", those who take illegal bets on sports, use cordless phones that operate up to one thousand feet from the phones. Other bookies have a variety of call forwarding services. Some even record bets on a water soluble rice paper for bets and instant burning flash paper so all evidence is easily destroyed in minutes if a police raid occurs. It is my opinion that they feel paper shreds can be reconstructed if given time so paper is used that can be easily destroyed.

Conclusion
When it comes to destroying paper, there is no hope of reconstruction if the paper is water soluble rice paper or instant burning flash paper. However; shredded paper can be reassembled.

When you consider the time and effort needed to assemble a shredded paper document and the fact that it is a tedious and boring process, it is best to get a professional. If the reassembled document is going to be used as evidence in a court of law, it might be best to use the professional service because they are going to have an expert that can most likely qualify as an expert witness through the "voir dire" process [4]. It is possible that the amateur document reconstruct personnel using manual techniques and scotch tape may alter the evidence to a degree that it is seriously challenged as admissible evidence in a court of law.

REFERENCES

1. Jacobs, J., Clemmer, L., Dalton, M., Posluns, J., (2003)," SSCP, Systems Security Practitioner Study Guide, Syngress Publishing, ISBN 1-931836-80-9, Page 149
2. Mitchell, C., Stone, M., Miller, J., (2002),"The Cell", Audio Book, An imprint of Simon Schuster, ISBN 0-7435-2014-9
3. URL Visited August 11,2005, www.DahlePaperShredders.com Phone number 1-800-992-5279
4. Smith, F., Bace., R., (2002),"A Guide to Forensic Testimony", Published by Addison Wesley, Page 8,9,276 - ISBN 0-201-75279-4
5. URL visited August 19,2005 http://www.ipsn.org/lolli2.html

Chapter 17 –
SIP Technology and the Tele-Robotic Arm –

Written by Joel Fernandes & coauthored by Dr. Doherty and edited by G. Stephenson

17.0 – Introduction

In this chapter we will examine a technology known as Session Initiation Protocol (SIP). It's generally thought in the telecommunication sector that SIP technology may play a big part in telephony, and allow people to make inexpensive phone calls. However a young man named Joel Fernandes demonstrated that SIP technology can also be used on the Internet as well as local networks to control a robotic arm. Joel created his own Visual C++ interface with buttons and a video interface so that he could create control signals to operate the robotic arm via the SIP technology. This system, when combined with a Cyberlink mental interface or Don Johnston sensor switch, had the potential to allow disabled persons to use a laptop and Internet connection to operate a robotic arm from anywhere on earth. Joel's senior honor's program thesis on SIP controlled robotic arms is a public document and is not considered a trade secret or anything patented.

The reader should know that Joel Fernandes is a young man who earned a B.S degree in Computer Science from Fairleigh Dickinson University in Teaneck, New Jersey in the United States in the Spring of 2004 and will soon complete a master's degree in the same discipline. While in college, Joel was on Channel 50 New Jersey News demonstrating a walking robot he modified with wireless video feed to allow paralyzed people to explore their home. Joel has also been interviewed by the newspaper on several occasions for his assistive technology efforts to help those with both cognitive and physical disabilities to recreate, communicate, and better interact with their environment.

This chapter will look at a new technology called Session Initiation Protocol (SIP), which can be used for telerobotic applications for both the civilian and military communities. Few people are aware of the flow of ideas and products that cross over between the disabled community and the military. I will now discuss a few examples of this migration of ideas and technology. I have a giant trackball known as "the Kids Ball" and that device is designed for young children to use to move a cursor on the screen. However; I have performed experiments in my doctoral degree at the University of Sunderland in England that showed how the trackball was useful for many people with cerebral palsy and cognitive impairments [4]. A professor in England told me during my studies as a doctoral student that he believed that trackballs that appeared similar were used in the first Gulf War with military avionics systems. Large thick handles for knives and items to be carried, originally seen on items for disabled people, are now seen on various types of military hardware. Military hydration systems with tubes that go into the mouth were once seen on soldiers engaged in desert warfare. Now such systems are seen on disabled persons with paralysis who need frequent fluid replenishment.

Please do not confuse the term "dual use" with the migration of ideas. "Dual use" is a term that we see in the media and is also used in books describing world politics such as the book called "Against All Enemies." [5] An example of dual use is when a company that appears to make aspirin for civilians could also be making components of a chemical warfare agent at the same time since the processes, skills, and equipment needed are reported to be quite similar. The migration of ideas is when a product that is made for one community is licensed to another industry that modify the original concept or application, to serve a completely different set of clients or for a different purpose. We will first examine the potential military uses for a SIP technology telerobotic system and then discuss the civilian uses. It is noteworthy that the prototype of the robot we use is plastic. However; similar looking industrial robotic arms with more durability and precision are available for sale if the military wished to make a real system out of the prototype we developed.

17.0.1 – Potential Military Uses for the SIP Telerobotic Arm System

Dr. Doherty simulated a disabled person as he wore an electrode on his forehead at the Fort Monmouth New Jersey Homeland Security Conference on June 7, 2004 and demonstrated Joel Fernandes' SIP Interface to operate a robotic arm. Prof. Doherty was able to visualize the type of work we wished to perform and then cognitively separated the task into small steps that could be carried out by the robotic arm. Lifting an object and moving it across the table would require him to first cognitively disassemble the task into such steps such as moving the robotic arm to the right, opening the pincers, lifting the shoulder of the arm up, moving it right, lowering it on the object, moving the wrist left or right, and squeezing the pincers on the object. Then the opposite set of steps would be done to move the object back to its starting location using the robotic arm.

Perhaps some of the people at the Homeland Security Conference of NJ speculated that a more robust version of the Session Initiation Protocol (SIP) telerobotic arm system could be used by the United States Army in urban warfare situations where unexploded ordinance (UXO) technicians had a hand injury and could not physically apply their expertise to neutralize an improvised explosive device (IED). Better versions of a SIP telerobotic arm system could perhaps allow a non-skilled soldier to place such a system near an IED and flee the area. Then as long as there was a wireless signal of sufficient strength, a link to the operator of the robotic arm could be established, and help the operator to maneuver the arm to snip a wire, or add a chemical to make the device inert. The operator of the robotic arm system only needs his or her eyesight, facial muscle control, and cognition to operate such a system which would allow for those severely injured to potentially save the lives of innocent children and senior citizens who may be nearby and unable to flee.

The idea of U.S. Army personnel being seriously injured during critical work became part of the public's consciousness in the movie, "Black Hawk Down" where a soldier loses a hand during urban warfare [1]. In the movie, we see that the soldier puts the severed hand in a pocket for later reattachment and uses his non dominant hand to complete his task to save the lives of his fellow Americans and reduce injury to civilians. Perhaps a soldier or civilian contractor whose job is to destroy UXO, could still stay an active member of the team and use an industrial mobile telerobotic arm system with a laptop and electrode on the forehead to disarm IEDs.

Joel Fernandes, Dr. Doherty, Gary Stephenson, and some of the people who discussed the uses of the telerobotic arm are not military personnel nor medical professionals. We have the creative minds of scientists and can propose various ideas but it will be the marketplace that will ultimately find the best use of SIP technology and telerobotic arms. We also think that the plethora of television channels, available movies, affordable books, and numerous internet articles have exposed us to many ideas and expanded our horizons of how we think about technology. It was President Reagan that once said that watching old movies is something that the world has in common and if he were here today he would probably say the same thing about the Internet too.

Figure 17.0.1 - Picture of Jeff Marsh Operating an Early Prototype of a Robotic Arm that Later Became Telerobotic

General Claudia Kennedy discusses in her book, "Generally Speaking" that the United States Army is becoming more high tech and specialized [2]. We can follow her career in the book and learn that she goes to NSA Cryptography School, Military Intelligence School, and receives other forms of training that takes years of expensive training to acquire. We can also imagine that a UXO technician goes to various training schools to learn to dissemble various types of improvised explosive devices, landmines, and unexploded ordinance from rocket propelled grenades as well as artillery. This training is expensive and the Army, with its limited budget and personnel, obviously can only train so many people. We get the idea that any advanced military occupation has a very finite supply of adequately trained people at anytime and such people take time and money to replace. These specialties play an important part in various operations so it is our opinion that it can be crucial to still keep an injured party working if possible, by utilizing their tacit knowledge, to help continue to save military and civilian lives.

General Claudia Kennedy also says that the future of warfare is not large armies coming together as in the cold war but from small urban warfare situations where the enemy is in an urban area filled with civilians. General Kennedy's book creates the impression that the Army is currently transforming itself to this new lightweight fast moving force that can pinpoint increased lethality on select targets and minimize civilian collateral damage. In spite of all the sophisticated armor and automated systems, it is still the human soldier who is still fragile. We can also conceptualize from movies such as "Black Hawk Down" how easy it is to get injured in an urban warfare situation such as Mogadishu even with all the body armor and armored vehicles. The point is that it appears that it is necessary to have systems that keep the limited personnel with important specialties working because often there are not replacements available. That specialty may be critical to getting the job done quickly and reducing chances those civilians nearby will get hurt.

A lot of grandparents and small children may be too frail to travel so getting the job done fast would seem important. Perhaps a portable telerobotic system much more durable and precise than our prototype could potentially enable the IED, UXO technician to stay on the job longer applying his or her expertise to disarm explosive devices and protect both civilians and military personnel. Everyone wants to reduce the unnecessary suffering to civilians.

17.0.2 – Legal Considerations that Impede Development of a SIP Telerobotic System

Homeland Security conferences such as the one at Fort Monmouth on June 7, 2004 can allow universities to show working conceptual proof of a prototype system such as the SIP telerobotic system for use in allowing injured soldiers or civilians to operate a robotic arm in their work. However; because of the lack of resources which includes funding and personnel, we have made our systems often at our own expenses and in our own time by modifying toy robotic arms such as the OWI-007. It is up to the private sector to implement our prototype because we can only speculate on a perceived need, create a proof of concept prototype, and present it. There is great expense in taking such a system to market with durable precision parts and hiring a patent lawyer to protect it, and establishing security protocols for keeping the code secret. There is also further expense in having proper insurance to deal with the liability in case of catastrophic product failure when used in battle causing the death or dismemberment of both military personnel and civilians.

There is legislation that the U.S. Congress passed in 2002 known as the safety act which put a cap on liability for Homeland Security type products. This Safety Act protection provides the consumer with only $250,000 of product liability but it is said to be very time consuming, difficult, and aggravating to obtain. The application process alone takes 120 days. There are also three conditions a vendor / developer must prove in order to get this safety act protection. The first requirement for the designation is to provide proof that the company would not provide its service or product without the safety act designation. The second requirement is that the company has to provide some insurance for the product but that cost cannot be completely passed on to the consumer. The third requirement is that the company must provide proof its product is ready to be manufactured and distributed. [3]

17.1 – The Academic's Dilemma when Developing the SIP Telerobotic System

The academic that is in a tenure track position at nearly any university is expected to write journal articles, present papers at conferences, and publish books. There are often administrators and colleagues at various educational institutions who push the academic to patent new technologies too. If the professor patents the technology, it is my opinion as a non legal professional, that he can no longer email work across borders with colleagues in other countries on developing source code because that would be exporting patented technology and would probably violate Title 18 United States Code Section 1832 which is a federal law punishable by up to five years in prison. When a federal sentence is pronounced, the entire sentence must be served. It is not commuted early for good behavior.

It is the opinion of Dr. Doherty that if one cannot write about technology in detail for conference papers and books, one is probably not fulfilling tenure requirements. It is the opinion of Dr. Doherty that both academics and graduate students need an area of research to work on for public disclosure in conferences, papers, and books while also having another area of research and development for patenting, working with the military or law enforcement, and not disclosing. It is the opinion of Dr. Doherty that intellectual property, rules on exporting technology, and rules for developing technology products between people of different nations needs much explanation to people throughout universities, private industry, and scientists of various nations to ensure that there are no gray areas. It is the opinion of Dr. Doherty that there are so many new laws and regulations that are ever changing or developing without our awareness which leads me to believe there needs to be more education on these topics so people can do things legally and without putting their organization or personal liberty at risk.

17.2 – Cognitive Aspects of Perform Work

Dr. Gilbert Cockton of the University of Sunderland, an esteemed professor in the discipline of human computer interaction, had said to me during my doctoral studies that the grouping of a collection of commonly used steps to perform a task was known as "chunking." It got me thinking of the task such as feeding myself, and all the steps that it took to accomplish this act myself. Then I performed what is known in England as a "cognitive walkthrough [6]" and thought of all the movements I had to do to move my shoulder, arm, wrist, fingers, and food to eat a fried chicken nugget for example. The convolution of a task into various steps was how I would teach disabled users to think about tasks before performing the work with either the telerobotic arm or robotic arm.

The other option for performing work was to have the robotic arm, the object of the work, and the user in the exact same spot and use a batch command so that the disabled person activated one button on the screen and the arm would move to set locations pick up the object and move it back. However this was not an option. Once while testing the robotic arm with students and cookies, a student had an automated system that allowed a quadriplegic man named Bruce Davis, to pick up a cookie and bring it up to feed himself. Bruce was not in the exact location and the cookie was close to his mouth but he could not reach it. Automated batch commands require the precise location of everything. In college in the 1980s I once rummaged through my pockets and wallet to get coins out to put it in a vending machine for coffee. The cup fell a few centimeters to the right and the coffee, milk, and sugar missed the cup and went in the drain. I was so upset that I wasted my money and the processed failed because one item, the cup, was not in its proper position. Then the door then opened up for me to grab the empty cup. Many vending machines for coffee now allow the door to be opened before the coffee is served to manually adjust the cup. It is a better design.

You now understand my dislike of the automated batch system for various mechanical systems.

We then created a manual control system for the telerobotic arm. Our menu for the telerobotic arm had commands for each degree of freedom for the robotic arm. That means base left, base right, shoulder up, shoulder down, elbow up, elbow down, wrist left, wrist right, pincers open, and pincers close. We then had to teach the user to perform work by performing a series of steps.

17.3 Joel Fernandes Motivation for the SIP Telerobotic Arm
The working telerobotic arm was demonstrated at the Northeast Regional Conference of the National Collegiate Honors Council, Hartford, CT, at Cybertherapy, San Diego, CA and at the Homeland Security Conference, Fort Monmouth, NJ. It was designed to allow disabled (paralyzed or quadriplegic) individuals to perform useful tasks over distances, eliminating their need for travel and possibly providing employment. The project has both hardware and software components that interact through the medium of the internet. Such a project can be expanded to include work in hazardous environments as speculated on earlier. The software, working in the Microsoft Windows environment operates a robotic arm (OWI-007) through the internet. Using Session Initiation Protocol (SIP) technology, a protocol developed for Voice over IP applications and incorporated in Microsoft's Real Time Communications Software Development Kit (SDK), provided feasible and successful means for transmission of commands to the robot. The application was built with client/server technologies that were present in late 2004 when Joel chose this project as my Senior Honors Thesis.

17.3.1 Technical Description of the Project
The Programming Environment was Microsoft Visual C++.NET.

The Platform was Windows XP Professional SP1.

The Robot was the OWI-007 Robotic Arm Kit,

Sensors: Don Johnston Sensor Switch/Switch Interface

Computers: Minimum 1 Ghz Processor (Intel Pentium III or equivalent), 256MB RAM

Video: 640x480 or higher (VGA) USB Camera

17.4 -An Introduction to SIP

Session Initiation Protocol (SIP) is a peer to peer solution to initiate a voice, video or data call over a TCP/UDP network. It is flexible and extensible, requiring one or more SIP Servers, which could be a proxy server or a registrar. The SIP registrar stores the location information of the client and therefore allows device portability across the network. During testing of the telerobotic arm project, a free version of Fomine Real Time Communication Server was used. It does the job of the registrar. Later we discovered yet another SIP Server solution, the OnDo SIP Server from Brekeke which provides a few additional features.

The overall system architecture for implementation of the test system is shown in the figure 17.2. Instead of the router/local network shown below, a high speed broadband internet connection may be substituted. For the purposes of operating a prototype telerobotic arm, we just required one SIP Server, two computers and a local intranet. (Alternately, the SIP Server software could run on the PC connected to the robot which would transmit the video stream to the client laptop, thereby cutting costs.)

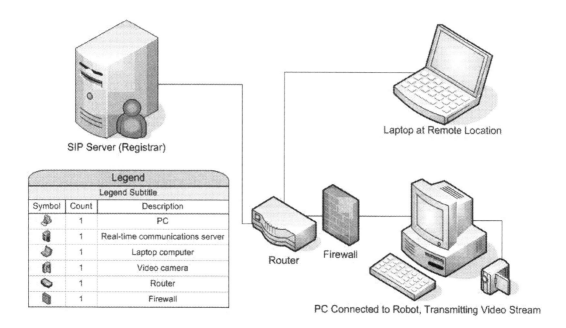

Legend		
Legend Subtitle		
Symbol	Count	Description
	1	PC
	1	Real-time communications server
	1	Laptop computer
	1	Video camera
	1	Router
	1	Firewall

Figure 17.2 - System Architecture

Let us zoom in a little into this functional overview to get an idea of what goes on behind the scenes. In this telerobotic project, applications makes function calls to Microsoft's Real Time Communications API, which in turn transforms these calls into the SIP Protocol messages which are then sent to the SIP Server and a session is negotiated between the two applications.

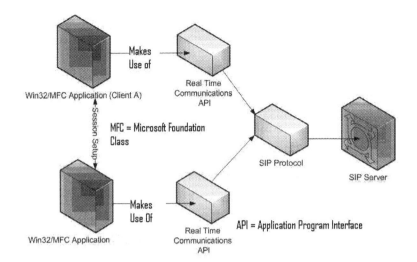

Figure 17.3: Data Transfer/Negotiating a Session

Though open source applications exist which utilize the SIP Protocol, the application that was created to control the robot over the internet uses Real Time Communications Client Application Programming Interface (API). A Software Development Kit (SDK) is available from the Microsoft Developer Network (http://www.msdn.com). The SDK comes with sources which can be compiled and a few sample applications. Programming in C++ and using the API requires knowledge of COM (Component Object Model). A discussion of COM Programming is rather long and tedious and in the realm of lengthy text books. An introduction can be found on MSDN at: (accessed September 15, 2005) http://msdn.microsoft.com/library/default. asp?url=/archive/en-us/directx9_c_summer_03/directx/intro/program/com/whatiscom.asp

The RTC COM object can be thought of as a base class with many interfaces. It is responsible for creating a session and then adding participants to that session. Specific to each interface are function calls, much like a class implementation in C++. The basic "connection" between two computers requires one to (in the program code) initialize the RTC object, create and enable a profile, create a session, register to receive events, handle events and make/terminate a call. More complicated functionality involves showing video and perhaps manipulating codecs (audio and video) to improve quality. Let's provide a few C++ "blurbs" or code-snippets which try to explain how some of the above is achieved.

The following lines sets up a pointer to the RTC Interface, creates the COM object and assigns a pointer to it. Normally you would store the return value of CoCreateInstance for error checking purposes:

```
IRTCClient *pIRTCClient;          //Pointer to the Client Interface

CoCreateInstance(CLSID_RTCClient, NULL, CLSCTX_INPROC_SERVER, IID_
IRTCClient, reinterpret_cast<void **>(&pIRTCClient));
```

```
/*
```

CoCreateInstance is quite standard in COM programming to create an instance of the COM Object and assign the pointer to it. If successful it returns a HRESULT value of S_OK. If the pointer was retrieved successfully, we can call

```
*/
```

pIRTCClient->Initialize();

Logging in to the SIP Server requires creating a provision, and subsequently a profile (such as a buddy name). Creating a provision requires some knowledge of XML.

Here is a code-snippet of what the XML provision would look like:

"<provision key=\"%s\" name=\"TeleROB\">"
"<user uri=\"%s\" account=\"%s\" name=\"%s\" password=\"%s\" realm=\"%s\" />"
"<sipsrv addr=\"%s\" protocol=\"%s\" %s role=\"registrar\">"
"<session party=\"first\" type=\"pc2pc\" />"
"<client name=\"%s\" />"
"</sipsrv>""</provision>"

Once the user is logged in, a call is made by first creating a session, then adding a participant and finally notifying the participant(s). The notifications, messages and media are all channeled through the SIP protocol. Shown below is an overview of what the protocol stack looks like. (RFC 2543) Voice and video is transmitted through Real Time Protocol (RTP). Real Time Control Protocol manages Quality of Service (QoS) and consists of messages sent periodically. RTCP messages hold information such as jitter, packets lost or dropped and any other condition relating to the flow of real time data. For example, if the bandwidth is not enough to transmit a smooth video stream, it will negotiate and switch to a lower quality codec.

Using Ethereal, a network packet sniffing software, it is possible to retrieve what a SIP message would look like.

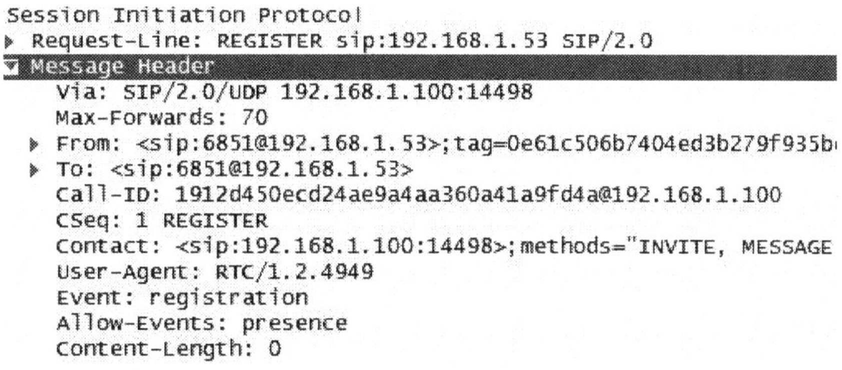

```
Session Initiation Protocol
▶ Request-Line: REGISTER sip:192.168.1.53 SIP/2.0
▼ Message Header
    Via: SIP/2.0/UDP 192.168.1.100:14498
    Max-Forwards: 70
  ▶ From: <sip:6851@192.168.1.53>;tag=0e61c506b7404ed3b279f935b
  ▶ To: <sip:6851@192.168.1.53>
    Call-ID: 1912d450ecd24ae9a4aa360a41a9fd4a@192.168.1.100
    CSeq: 1 REGISTER
    Contact: <sip:192.168.1.100:14498>;methods="INVITE, MESSAGE
    User-Agent: RTC/1.2.4949
    Event: registration
    Allow-Events: presence
    Content-Length: 0
```

Figure 17.4: SIP Packet (Captured with Ethereal)

Besides these SIP messages, there are also SDP (Session Description Protocol) messages that are transmitted between client and server. These packets allow client/server to negotiate compatible voice/video (media) codecs based on available bandwidth, quality, traffic, compatibility and considerations for that session.

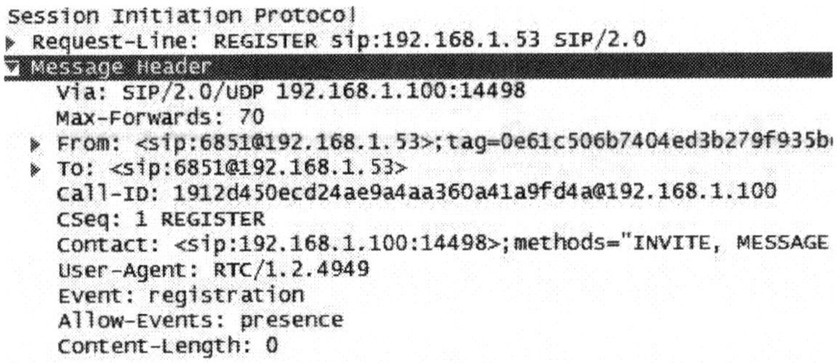

```
Session Initiation Protocol
▶ Request-Line: REGISTER sip:192.168.1.53 SIP/2.0
▽ Message Header
    Via: SIP/2.0/UDP 192.168.1.100:14498
    Max-Forwards: 70
  ▶ From: <sip:6851@192.168.1.53>;tag=0e61c506b7404ed3b279f935b
  ▶ To: <sip:6851@192.168.1.53>
    Call-ID: 1912d450ecd24ae9a4aa360a41a9fd4a@192.168.1.100
    CSeq: 1 REGISTER
    Contact: <sip:192.168.1.100:14498>;methods="INVITE, MESSAGE
    User-Agent: RTC/1.2.4949
    Event: registration
    Allow-Events: presence
    Content-Length: 0
```

Figure 17.5: SDP Packet (Captured with Ethereal)

REFERENCES

1. "Black Hawk Down", 144 Minutes, Made by Columbia Pictures, (2002), ISBN 0-7678-7062-X
2. Kennedy, C., (2001),"Generally Speaking", Abridged version for books on tape, Time Warner Audio Books, ISBN 1-58621-175-7
3. Grasser, E., (2005), "Safety Act Process", Security Management, March 2005, An ASIS International Publication, Page 20
4. Doherty, E., (2001), "An Investigation of Bio-Electric Interfaces For Computer Users with Disabilities",Doctoral Thesis, University of Sunderland, Page 32
5. Clarke, R., (2004), "Against All Enemies", ISBN 0-7435-3637-1
6. Hill, S., (1995), "The Human Computer Interface", ISBN 1-85805-119-3, Published in London by DP Publications Ltd., Page 120

General References
- "Session Initiation Protocol"
  - http://www.cs.columbia.edu/~hgs/sip (accessed: 05/04/05)

- "SIP Tutorial
  - http://www.iptel.org (accessed: 05/01/05)
- "Microsoft Real Time Communications Client SDK"
  - http://www.msdn.com
- Minoli, D. and Minoli, E., "Delivering Voice over IP Networks", Second Edition

ALL IMAGES IN THIS CHAPTER WERE DEVELOPED IN MICROSOFT VISIO 2003 by JOEL FERNANDES

Chapter 18 –
Alternate Methods of Powering & Using the Network
When Disaster Strikes

18.0 – Introduction

I started to think about what would happen if there was a large scale disaster when I visited rural Georgia in the late 1990s. Many people used to emergency preparations due to bad weather were using a similar strategy for preparing for the Y2K bug. This appeared to be a good approach since electricity and refrigeration could be affected. Some people familiar with principles of emergency management were putting away supplies of dried food, bottled water, and many purchased a generator so they could operate a TV or radio in order to listen to emergency broadcasts and news to stay informed. Others with small children felt a refrigerator was important for certain baby foods.

There was even talk around the entire nation about the power grid being affected by the Y2K bug. For anyone who does not remember, there was a lot of doom and gloom predicted because computer systems were reported to be unequipped to handle the change from 1999 to 2000. People in every sector were worried how service oriented billing would handle calculating power consumption for example if the program only used the last two digits of the year. There were even small followings of people on the Internet predicting world doom.

Some people in New Jersey were buying dried food and bottled water too. Others were buying generators for power and thinking of safe ways to store large amounts of fuel. There was a lot of talk that the power grid would be affected and there might be a lot of chaos if traffic lights were not functioning. It seemed like a good thing that people were planning for how they would cope for the loss of telephone service, Internet, and electricity. Richard Gigliotti has a book called Emergency Planning for Maximum Protection that has a chapter that helps anyone prepare a plan for large scale events [1]. The Y2K (year 2000) problem really never happened as predicted in my opinion simply because network administrators, software developers, and town administrators took a proactive approach to the potential problem and hired consultants to fix the problem.

I feel that the minimal impact of the Y2K bug was due to a unified quiet effort between private industry and various levels of government that allowed systems to be fixed off online and then put online after proper testing that allowed a smooth transition into the new millennium. This partnership worked even before the Department of Homeland Security was created and shows how people can work together proactively to avoid a crisis.

18.1 – Packet Switched Networks and the Philosophy of Decentralized Networks

I have an amateur radio license and therefore have a right to use certain frequencies for digital communication that others without a license cannot use. I will now tell you a story about a packet network I used in 1992-1993 because it combines computers, radio frequencies, and the

Internet. You may think it is no big deal but it was 10 years before wireless networks became publicly available to the average consumer in the United States.

I enjoyed setting up my Radio Shack 2 meter VHF radio with my computer and connecting it to my terminal node controller (TNC). I also used the Radio Shack linear amplifier to boost my signal. Then I used a directional antenna that looked similar to a long TV antenna. It was on top of a 20 foot pole which I spun around by rotor until a storm burned it out. Then I later had to go in the yard and turn it and shout to my father who sat by the computer near the window. He would tell me when text with call signs and messages flashed across the screen. I connected two towns away to Chuck's packet radio network at his home. He was probably less than 10 miles as the crow flies but there were many mountains that blocked the signals.

I once dug a hole that was four feet deep and put in a plastic PVC pipe with a diameter of 3 inches.Then my father and I put in a small bag of dirt. Then we took cut logs of few inches thick and tamped the ground. Then we poured in more dirt. Then we tamped it with the wood. Then later I jumped up and down on the dirt to compress it. Then we put down more dirt and tamped it. A neighbor had once got rid of a solid steel 20 foot pole they used as a railing and gave it to me. I had put the antenna on top of the pole with clamps. It took two people to lift it. When a large antenna is on top of a 20 foot pole, even a small movement is amplified and balance can be easily lost and the whole thing comes down. Once you get the pole up you have to walk with it and balance it. Then you have to drop it in the sleeve which is the buried pipe. That was my antenna system. Some years later a neighbor who was a ham radio operator gave me a rotor system. That was big and heavy and looked like a truck transmission. It was even harder to get the pole back in the hole after this heavy rotor and antennas were on it.

When I had first got my ham radio license, I got a topographic map which showed the elevations and hills in my area. It was possible to determine the best path or azimuth on paper to Chuck's Packet Radio at his house. Whenever you go from paper to compass readings outside in the real world in New Jersey there is about a 15 degree difference between north on the map and magnetic north. The difference is listed on topographic maps near the legend. It is different depending at what latitude you live at.

I would turn on the computer and go to the DOS and run the packet program. Then I would turn on the terminal node controller (TNC) and make sure it was plugged in my 9 pin serial port. Then the TNC was connected to the VHF radio. I would then use the rotor to turn the antenna until I saw traffic. Everything was text base and since the packets were sent over the air, I would estimate maximum speeds of 45 characters a minute appearing on my screen. It was a big deal to connect to a station a few towns away. My TNC and VHF radio were battery operated. My computer was on a large uninterruptible power supply (UPS), that was purchased from a military surplus sale from the local army base. The system could work for at least 20 minutes without outside power. This was in the early 1990s. My father and I once turned on the computer, the TNC, and turned on the radio to a preset frequency in the 145-150 megahertz range.

Then I used the JNOS operating system and would type c for connect and the call sign for Chuck's radio. If my dad and I did not connect, we adjusted the rotor until we started seeing a connection. Then there would be network traffic on the computer screen with call signs saying hello to me. Then I found a way to connect by radio to the computer system of a ham radio operator with a public packet station nearby. Then I connected via radio from his system to a computer in the vicinity of the George Washington Bridge. Then I connected through a dedicated line in the transatlantic cable to England. Then on a packet computer system in England we connected by high frequency radio to stations high in rural locations in Austria. It took about 3 seconds per letter to go from my screen to Austria. It was really slow. Once my dad and I sat at least an hour in a text conversation to a man named Oleg, who was on a trip near the North Pole. Perhaps he was looking for oil or natural gas. We were surprised his batteries were holding out on such a long trip.

The protocol used on the packet radio was AX.25. It was the same used in the Aloha Network used in the early 1970s [2]. Packet Radio was an extension of packet research used in the ARPANET by the Defense Advanced Research Project Agency (DARPA), which is the father of the modern Internet. ARPANET was a project to allow synchronous communications from a variety of sources without using a centralized location. You can see from ARPNET and the Aloha Net that there was an effort in the 1960s to decentralize communications so that if the cold war became a real war, the United States could still function if one critical area such as Washington was hit with a missile and critical telecommunications were disabled. Richard Clarke speaks in his book about activating COG, Continuance of Government after 9-11 [3]. It appears from the book that COG allows for government to continue by designating various people at various locations to perform government functions as opposed to the usual centralized locations. Richard Clarke also states there is a secure video conference center in one of the wings of the White House to communicate with remote sites for COG.

There were a variety of Internet links showing that the United States Army uses a Tactical Area Network that works on the principles of the old Aloha Net and packet radio. Such networks are in my opinion not useful in places such as Afghanistan because of the large mountains that block signals. I am thinking of the small hills where I live and the difficulty of such connections there. People may find packet networks useful in places where there is little existing infrastructure and relatively flat large open areas and stationary or slow moving vehicles. Wireless packets of computer text can easily pass low bandwidth text messages and could perhaps be encoded with GPS coordinates so all units know of each other's whereabouts.

18.2 – Uninterruptible Power Supplies, Gel Cells, Generators, Windmills
Some people like using laptops because they are portable and modern lithium laptop batteries often run three or four hours after charging. The laptop can also be used with a twelve volt connector in the car cigarette lighter. There are also twelve volt batteries known as "gel cells" which can provide power to radios and certain peripheral devices should the car not be available. There are also gasoline generators that are the size of a lawn mower which can provide additional power. There are a lot of options. Some people will only use portable

devices because of the small size and flexibility in options for power. Generators are often available at hardware stores while gel cells, and cigarette lighter adapters are available at places such as Radio Shack.

Many people are also spending approximately US$40 for small flashlights that use a hand generator instead of batteries. Such units also have a radio built in. A few turns of the crank will often provide a half hour of power. These are good because batteries often have a limited shelf life and people are often so busy they forget to replenish them. Many people I have met from first world countries are buying these units for relatives in developing nations where batteries are difficult to get.

Some radios and palmtops that use LCD displays and require low amperage are powered on sunny days by solar panels. Many times people will purchase a solar panel for US$200 and leave it connected to the unit so it provides what is known as a "trickle charge" to keep it fully charged. Perhaps Oleg used solar panels, a hand generator flashlight / radios and laptops on his trip in the Arctic. I did talk to a man on the 20 meter band of the ham radio in the Ukraine who once told me he took an alternator from a large truck and put it on a homemade windmill. The wind turned the windmill and spun the alternator and gave him enough power to use his radio and portable computer equipment.

18.3 – Special Input Devices for When Health A Crisis or Injury Arises

There are times when civilians get a brain injury, a stroke, or fall and break an arm. They can often no longer use a mouse effectively as they shake their hand from involuntary movements so that moving the cursor on a small icon is nearly impossible. There are various devices one can use to operate a cursor besides a mouse such as a trackball. Trackballs come in many sizes. Some really small trackballs are known as thumb balls because they are operated with the thumb on your dominant hand. Some trackballs made for children such as the "Kids Ball" have a big ball with nearly a 3 inch diameter. These trackballs worked well in experiments I performed in my days of doctorate studies because some people with mental and physical impairments could not operate a mouse at all but could operate a Kids Ball. The people in the experiments also liked the Kids Ball trackball because the button for clicking was an inch away from the way from the ball and the separation of the button from the ball was great because involuntary movements on the ball rarely affected the clicking button. The Kids Ball trackball is pictured in Figure 18.1.

Military personnel that have taken part in urban warfare are reported on television interviews to sustain many injuries in Humvees. We know this because there have been televised appeals for inventors to make homemade armor to put on the military vehicles. The homemade armor has been used by National Guard Units with personnel who were welders and civilian steel workers. Many soldiers in Humvees have been reported in other chapters to operate computerized network systems such as the FCBC2 Blue Force Tracking. FCBC2 shows real time maps of all friendly and enemy units and allow real time text chat between American and Coalition Forces. However; the military video shows everyone using a mouse.

Perhaps it would be good to also carry large trackballs in case hands or arms are injured by enemy fire and precise movements and simultaneous movements of hands and fingers are not possible. There is some very interesting literature by Swierenga and Struckman-Johnson that compares the mouse, trackball, and another common input device called a joystick [4]. When you read this literature, please take note to the condition of the people in the study. Perhaps you may want to read about a comparison of users with a variety of cognitive and physical impairments using such devices as in the Doherty doctoral thesis [6], or my book on the subject, *Computer Recreation for Everyone* (ISBN 1-4208-2239-X).

Injuries occur too frequently from household or automobile accidents, degenerative diseases, or from war. Regardless of the cause, the results are similar in that all such affected users of computer networks now need special accommodation. The type of accommodation depends on the type of injury. Blind users usually have no problem with hand movements and clicking but have no idea where they are moving the cursor unless there is an assistive technology to read the screen and give a clue to the location of the cursor. Users with paralysis and severe motor impairment may need an assistive technology such as sip and puff that scan items on the screen and selection is done by sipping on a tube. People with a brain injury and severe motor impairment due to diseases such as ALS that cause the person to decline in skills may find a Cyberlink brain body interface the way to allow the user more control of the cursor [5].

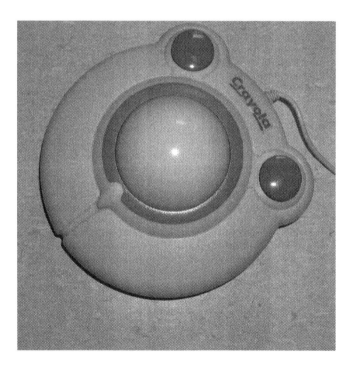

Figure 18.1 – A Large Trackball Similar to the Kid's Ball

REFERENCES

1. Gigliotti, R., Jason, R., (1991), "Emergency Planning for Maximum Protection", Butterworth-Heinemann Publishing, ISBN 0-409-90076-1
2. Mayo, J.,(1989),"The Packet Radio Handbook", Published by Tab Books, Page 20-21, ISBN 0-8306-3222-0
3. Clarke, R., (2004), "Against All Enemies", ISBN 0-7435-3637-1
4. Swierenga, S., Struckman-Johnson, D.,(1984),"Alternative Cursor Control Devices: An Empirical Comparison Using a Tracking Task (Final Report: Task II.3), Vermillion S.D., University of South Dakota, Human Factors Laboratory
5. URL Visited 2004 – www.brainfingers.com
6. Doherty, E., (2001), "An Investigation of Bio-Electric Interfaces For Computer Users with Disabilities", Doctoral Thesis, University of Sunderland, Page 32 - 40

Chapter 19 –
Counterfeiting and Personal Computers

19.0 – Introduction

There are some historical sources that report there was a lot of counterfeit bills in the Confederate States of America in the 1860s. Part of this could be opportunists from the North seeking goods for nothing or perhaps some people took it upon themselves to try to flood the South, namely the Confederate States of America, with phony bills to undermine confidence in the currency and destabilize the South and thus bring the war to a halt much quicker. The ending of the war would quickly both preserve the Union and preserve human life. Counterfeit bills can be used as a form of economic warfare or for criminal purposes, namely getting something for nothing.

In this chapter we will examine how counterfeiting has gone from an operation with master craftsman and large printing presses to grade school kids making phony bills on personal computers using inkjet printers.

19.1 – The Secret Service

There was such a flood of counterfeit bills during the Civil War that were of such high quality that many people in the South were reported to prefer the fakes over the real bills. The engravers who made such bills were prevalent and the problem of counterfeit money became such a problem that on July 5, 1865, the United States Government created the Secret Service. Chief William P. Wood was sworn in by the Treasury Department into the Secret Service [1]. The Secret Service is still active today when people try to counterfeit money. Sometimes today people will also try to alter historic coins such as an Indian Head penny. A date could be changed from the 1800s to be an 1877 date which can command hundreds to thousands of dollars. Some Indian Head pennies with the likeness of a chief can be bought for a dollar so changing the date can yield a large windfall profit for a counterfeiter. An Indian Head penny is visible in Figure 19.1

Figure 19.1 – Indian Head Penny 1877

19.2 – Super Hundred Dollar Bills

There is an excellent document that was issued from the United States General Accounting Office in the 1990s [2]. The document of interest is the "GAO/GGD-96-11 "Counterfeit U.S. Currency Abroad". This document suggests there is widespread high quality counterfeit currency production from places in the Middle East. There is concern that such counterfeit bills could undermine faith in the currency and be used as a type of "economic terrorism." This prompted the United States Government to redesign the hundred dollar bill so that it would have many security features built in so that it would be nearly impossible to pass off to a person trained to recognise these features on the bill that they received.

19.3 – Low Quality Fakes

High quality fakes must be part of a large operation with plates and master craftsman. Such craftsmen consider themselves to be artists and must use sophisticated equipment that can command sizeable costs that most small time criminals cannot afford. The small time thief will use a photocopier that does color copies because the result is reasonably high quality while the training needed is low. The equipment might be available at the copy store or used by deviant cleaning personnel at large corporation at night after hours. Expensive machines in corporations are often left unmanned for hours at night.

A newspaper in New Jersey called the Morris County Daily Record, known hereafter as "The Record", reports on this problem [3,5]. The Record reports that many low quality fakes will be passed by people when they see inexperienced clerks such as high school students besieged by busy crowds buying ice cream or anytime checking bills is nearly impossible because of the demand for service and the lack of service personnel. You could probably think of such opportunities for putting a fake bill in someone's hand and not having time to check it. Perhaps a busy gas station with three bays and one clerk would provide an opportunity, especially if the counterfeiter comes in with a female partner in a separate vehicle who is quite attractive and whose car needs attention, as a distraction

19.4 – Creating Fakes

The Record reports how a high number of fakes are being passed by people who just need a little "weekend fun money" or even kids who want to "pass off bills" for pizza at lunch time [5]. The tools of the trade appear to be a scanner and inkjet color printer. Within a day of the new bills reaching the public, I heard rumors in my community that some people were arrested passing phony bills at the local mall.

19.5 – Detecting Fakes

Higher quality fakes can be mass produced with a laser color printer but authorities can catch such people because if you hold a bill up to a purple light, the serial number can be embedded in the paper [4]. The number is not visible to the naked eye and regular lights will not expose it. Such purple lights can even be purchased at some hardware stores and are small enough to go on a keychain.

In another incident, a Madison, New Jersey detective sergeant named Dennis Lam noticed a man was carrying hundred dollar bills with all the same serial number [3]. Serial numbers should all be different and if a damaged bill is replaced, the replacement bill has a star at the end of the serial number indicating a reprint. Star notes are also highly desirable to coin collectors because of their rarity. Real twenty dollar bills have lifelike distinct lines where fakes don't. Twenties have embedded blue and red fibers, while fakes have little blue and red lines on the paper [5]. The twenty dollar bill is not made of bond paper from your local store but is a waterproof quality paper that is from a secret formula and process. The sad part is that I have heard rumors that some criminals will use methods to wash the ink off of the one dollar bill and use it to make a fake twenty.

19.6 – Federal Law Enforcement and Industry Stopping Counterfeiting

Now there is a "counterfeit deterrence system", that is built into various software packages and copy machines so that if one tries to copy money, a barking sound occurs and the process stops [5]. Money has a certain color code and when scanned, it can easily be detected. Some feel it might be a good idea if in the future a notification could be sent by your system to manufactures and police via the Internet if the barking feature was activated. Adobe Photoshop is set up to prevent people from scanning and printing money.

REFERENCES

1. URL Visited August 19,2005 http://www.secretservice.gov/history.shtml
2. URL Visited August 19,2005
   http://www.globalsecurity.org/security/library/report/gao/gg96011.pdf
3. McKnight, J., "Cops: Worker's money was funny", Morris County's Daily Record, Friday, August 19,2005
4. Tuohey, J, "Government Uses Color Laser Technology to Track Documents", PC World, http://pcworld.about.com/news/Nov222004id118664.htm
5. Locv, T., "Small Businesses Hit Hardest by Counterfeiters", Morris County's Daily Record, Friday, August 19,2005

Chapter 20 –
Creating a Conference of Security Professionals to Network with

20.0 Introduction to Creating a Conference

There is a point when a technology matures and there is a community that finds a new use for it, and then they create a conference to address the needs of that community. Let us apply this concept to a real life situation. Some years back there were two games that allowed people to play with friends or coworkers on a computer network. These games were called "Doom" and "Castle Wolfenstein." These games created a very realistic environment of a castle and one could go around and shoot monsters, other players, and collect objects of some value in the game. These castles were an example of virtual environments and provided a "place in cyberspace" where people could recreate, explore, and blow some steam off after a hard day at work. These virtual environments were known to some as "virtual reality" or VR. Most people into computers that I knew in the early to mid 90s enjoyed playing this game after work. It was absolutely fun. There were conferences in California for Virtual Reality (VR) that emphasized gaming.

Then other people who were psychologists and rehabilitation specialists saw that VR games of certain types could sometimes also be used for other purposes with people who had various physical or mental impairments. Perhaps games with virtual towns in them could be used to teach people to remember landmarks and navigate a community. Such skills could be useful after long stays in the hospital when people had to join the community again. Many professionals in the rehabilitation community, mental health community, and video game community went to the virtual reality conferences. These three communities had a common interest in building virtual environments though their purposes were different. However; their common interests in learning the language VRML to create virtual worlds for users to explore promoted an environment of mutual learning and support. Video gaming professionals and the wider health care community were also interested in input devices such as the head mounted displays that allowed users to be more immersed in the game as it became more realistic. Here we can see that although the technical interests were the same the purposes for the applications were different.

The video gaming community and health care communities even discussed topics such as Cyber sickness where a player might find themselves a bit queasy after playing a game, for instance when they were in a simulated airplane environment. Then there came a point where the processors became faster, the software matured, and the communities diverged. The rehabilitation community included a subset of individuals who wanted to create applications for fear of flying. They wanted simulations that were professional for their field of care. A flight simulator game where a plane could become out of control and crash is not in my lay opinion an acceptable option for people seeking help for fear of flying.

If you check on the Internet, you can now see a Conference called Cybertherapy with people who are interested in VR applications as a tool for licensed mental health care professionals to use in their treatment of phobias. Many of the people who attend Cybertherapy once attended the Virtual Reality conferences. We can see how a technology emerges, a diverse community emerges, and then another community spins off and forms a conference to address the needs of a new community of professionals. It is my opinion that a conference can address a particular need of professional individuals for a period of time. I feel conferences form a community of shared ideals, goals, and provide mutual support.

20.1 – Creating a Conference

So now we may have identified a niche market and a set of individuals who share a need for this market. You can get their emails, phone numbers, fax numbers, or addresses and contact them to tell them you wish to provide a conference in your area. If the conference addresses a local or regional set of professionals, then place the conference in that region. I once created an Academic Homeland Security conference for a university in the New Jersey area, so of course I held the conference in New Jersey to keep down costs and allow everyone to commute to it. However; once I created the conference, people from other countries and states said they wished to attend. This widened the focus a bit and I had to find a conference hotel for them.

20.2 – Location

The Cybertherapy group I used in my original example involves people from California, Canada, Israel, Switzerland, Korea, Columbia, and Spain. The conference has been in California, Switzerland, and will go to Canada so as to make it easier for various communities to travel too and thus lessen expenses. In such an international community of professionals, it is also being culturally sensitive to others to move the conference to countries where clusters of members reside. It also gives a everyone an opportunity to enjoy other cultures and see people in the context of their home community. For instance, I would enjoy the opportunity to see Madrid, watch Flamingo Dancing, see Andalusia, and see how computer applications are used in the Spanish Health Care System.

In the New Jersey conference example, if most people are commuting to the conference, parking is a big issue. Many communities that are urban such as Hoboken, have little if any parking on the street and multi-story parking garages often fill up and are expensive. You may want to find a location that has ample parking and is safe, lighted, and inexpensive. You must also consider a location where people are not getting ticketed for not running out and putting money in parking meters. If your population is ambulatory and not senior citizens, then a parking lot that is considerable distance from the conference might be ok, but you might want to have a shuttle and provide handicapped parking or for after dark.

20.3 – Conference Hotel

You really need to be sensitive to the economic needs of your conference attendees. If many people attending the conference are on limited fixed budgets, then you don't book the five star hotel because it will be out of the budget of most people. I once worked for a department at a school that gave me $1000 a year for conferences so I had to use my frequent flyer miles for the airfare, pay my own meals, and used the $1000 to pay the conference fee and hotel. I also felt the hotel was too fancy for my tastes and would have preferred more modest accommodations that were within my budget.

Then on the other side of the coin, I have met people at conferences that are really wealthy and a two star hotel might be "roughing it." I will give you an example of a wealthy attendee. One of my international students asked me to tie his tie before presenting to a group because he did not know how to tie a tie. He handed me a silk tie that he said was only $90 and told me one of his servants at home would tie his tie and he never learned though he was 30 years old. Many conference attendees may have common interests but are from diverse economic backgrounds and strata in society.

Selecting a conference hotel is a difficult task that takes careful consideration. You need to be sensitive to people's tastes and economics. The conference hotel needs to be in a location that is within reasonable distance to an airport and easy and affordable for attendees. If the hotel is 5 hours from the airport, it can lead to taxi drivers taking 7 hours to get there and potentially getting lost and causing people lost time and stress.

Sometimes the hotel can be really plush, inexpensive, and minutes from the airport, but the location is in a city that is a distraction. Las Vegas is inexpensive, has great food and accommodation, but the casinos can sometimes be of more interest to people than many of the conference sessions and this unwanted distraction can affect attendance at some sessions.

20.4 – Food

You also need to be sensitive to people's dietary needs for the local or remote conference. Religious restrictions often mean pork, bacon, and other meats may not be served. There should be a vegetarian option for people because of either health concerns or for those who are observing religious restrictions. A man I know who had heart surgery was forbidden by his doctor to eat any meats. Some people have food allergies and can get deathly ill from eating peanuts or from purines in foods such as asparagus or shellfish. Some people may take medicine for high blood pressure and take blood thinners that recommend they do not eat leafy vegetables with vitamin K. I think a sensitive and sensible way to approach the subject is to ask people if you can accommodate any special dietary needs. You also need to maintain people's privacy and accommodate their needs.

20.5 – Keynote Speaker

I was once at a computer interface conference in Seattle around the time of the new millennium and Bill Gates from Microsoft was the keynote speaker. The extra security needed made it seem like (POTUS) the "President of the United States" was there. The extra security was costly and you never knew if such an important person would bring activists or security concerns. Other people were focusing on wanting to talk to Bill about things they wanted to see added to Windows or address concerns they had with Microsoft products. I felt it was a distraction much like having a conference in Las Vegas.

I would have rather have seen a more low key speaker that did not require special security and all that added expense. A lower key speaker would allow people to focus on the more mundane themes of the conference as opposed to people seeking an audience with "Bill." Too low key a speaker means many people will not attend. It is a fine balancing act.

Occasionally, a keynote speaker that is really controversial may be invited and this might cause a rift in the conference and create stress as people polarize into factions. One really needs to be sensitive to people's needs and get someone that addresses a technology need or moves people in the field in a unifying positive direction. It is best to have a "focus group" as President Clinton used to say or a committee of people who represent your field and discuss it with them. The conference director needs to be open to the advice of the committee.

20.6 – Vendors

It is often good to invite vendors because people may not have the time to read all the trade journals of their chosen field and are unaware of the quality products that are out there. I was at two security related conferences once and people told me they were unaware that there was a machine that you could purchase and install on your premises that could blow air all around you and get trace samples of materials that could be potentially either narcotics or explosives. I walked past a machine called the "Sentinel 2." It took only a short time, a fraction of a minute, and it blew air all around me. I was "ok" and walked threw it. I only heard of the "puffer" as it is called in slang and did not know it was operational. Perhaps someone would add this device to their perimeter security plan at their access control points. It is difficult to balance the need for vendors to show products in your field, be it network security or physical security, and not be endorsing those products for a hard sell. Vendors carry products for sale to meet real or imagined needs are in my opinion where reality meets the perceived wants and needs of that particular community.

20.7 – Sharing Ideas and Moving Ahead in History

We know humans are social beings and have come together on an annual or semiannual basis for dozens of generations. In Western culture, places such as Stonehenge or New Grange for example have served as sort of an outdoor conference center where people have collectively shared ideas and tools for millennia. Some scientists speculate that Stone Age people and Bronze Age people met and shared tools and ideas at Stonehenge. The Stone Age people then accepted many of these new tools and ideas and transitioned ahead to the Bronze Age. My point is that human communities have shared tools and ideas even before the written recording of history. In the end, the more advanced tools and ideas are adopted and the way we carry on business and daily living is changed. It is known as the marketplace of ideas.

In Ancient Greece, Pythagoras and other mathematicians would frequently meet and discuss math and theorems, especially the relationship between the sides of the triangle. Eventually the Pythagorean Theorem was adopted. A mathematic community in China also discussed the relationship of the sides of the triangle in a famous paper document called, "The Problem of the Broken Bamboo" by Yang Hui in 1261 [1]. The Plimpton 322 stone tablet of Ancient Babylon (1900 -1600 B.C.) was a document that showed various values of three sides of triangles and some parametric equations for a, b, and c [2]. We see again that there were conferences of mathematicians that got together and advanced science and improved upon the Pythagorean Theorem with parametric equations. Each generation of scientists, technologists, and mathematicians stands on the shoulders of the generation before it. Ideas have always traversed from East to West and vice versa along the silk route through Central Asia.

20.8 – The Importance of Documents and the Advancing of Science

It is important in network security, telerobotics, or any other discipline to move ahead. The conference or gathering of people need to share and disseminate their ideas orally, by stone document, by paper document, or in the digital format on a PowerPoint slide allows us to discuss current policies, procedures, tools, theories, and suggest new tools for new problems. It is the sharing of problems and the discussion to seek new solutions that move any discipline ahead. We saw that the ancient Babylonians and Stone Age people expressed ideas in stone documents. Some ideas were passed on by word of mouth as with Pythagoras. Many great Chinese ideas and modern ideas in science are passed on in the exchange of papers. In the last few years many papers and ideas are passed in digital format by PowerPoint slides by both email and the Internet. It is my opinion that only the medium of idea transmission has changed. We went from spoken ideas, to written ideas in stone, to written ideas on paper, to the latest medium, which is a digital format. What will be next?

The stone document is heavy to move and requires people to be physically present. That means that the transmission of ideas among communities would be slow in the stone age. Ideas that were more complex and on paper could be copied by scribes and passed around on ships or by horse and buggy. This would be faster than stone but not as fast as in the digital age. Now the transmission of ideas and the sharing and discussion of ideas is instantaneous in the digital age. It is my opinion that volatile ideas can travel too fast and cause friction between people. Conferences again allow a community that shares a common discipline to meet either in person or in a virtual format on the web and share ideas orally, digitally, or on paper and the best ideas are kept after debating and thus advance science. Poor ideas are simply dead ends on the idea family tree.

20.9 – Conference Proceedings

The conference proceedings may show some of the best papers and ideas of that time as well as the debates, activities, and people present in that field. They serve as an archive of where that community was at a given point in time. If the conference is in telerobotics, we can look at the proceedings in the future and see what stage the technology was at that time as well as the ideas of that community at that time. We can see some of the leaders in that community and see a marketplace of ideas and what moved ideas on and what ones stopped. The human family also has produced some offshoots in evolution that went nowhere. In the human family we know that Neanderthal man and Cro Magnon man where branches that stopped. Unlike the human family, in the family tree of ideas, we can always look back and examine the ideas that did not move forward and see if they had any merit and are worth revisiting.

REFERENCES

1. Eves, H., (1984),"An Introduction to the History of Mathematics", Saunders College Publishing, Fifth Edition, Page 160, ISBN 0-03-062064-3
2. Eves, " ", page 28

Chapter 21 –
Wireless Security and Other Non Related Security Topics

21.0 Introduction to Wireless Security and Non Related Tips
This chapter discusses a lot of security tips you can investigate to increase your wireless security. I did not say it will prevent break-ins. It will improve your security if you use these tips, especially if you have not done so previously. You should not change any configurations on your router / switch unless you are the owner; your Internet Service Provider allows it in the policy, and you accept all risks of changing settings. The purpose of this chapter is to help you understand some wireless security techniques that you might use as part of a vulnerability assessment.

The other part of the chapter is to just put a lot of unrelated security items together because they might be of interest to you and I did not know where else to put them. We all meet a myriad of people in our lives and learn bits and pieces from them. Some bits may be eccentricities, some have little value, and some illustrate concepts of information security that can be applied and hopefully be of some value. It is up to you to separate the wheat from the chaff. Hopefully you will find more wheat than chaff. Here are a lot of bits and bobs first before we get to our wireless security.

21.1 – Names and Information Security
There was an old man I knew many years ago and we will call him "Jack." His real name is not of any importance anyway since he was not famous and has long since passed on. I liked talking to Jack occasionally because he had interesting stories and saw right through the "worthless talk" many people throw around and "had everyone's number" so to speak. Jack was a real quiet fellow and very low key. He had an electronic test equipment sales office in his basement and only a couple people in his neighborhood knew about it. One time I saw all these badges with Jack's picture and various last names like "Wallensky", or "Greginsky" but they always had his correct first name. I asked what was going on. He told me when he went to various conferences, he used different names and would track the name from the time of the conference to junk mail to telemarketers. He kept a list of each name and where it went. He wanted to see who sold his name and how the trail progressed. I thought that was fascinating but useless information.

Jack was cleaning out his basement and needed my help. I collected some magazines and scrap paper from him and would take it to recycling so it would not fill up his garbage and be too heavy for the garbage men. Recycling was not in vogue in the early 80s but I thought it was good for the environment. Jack told me to stop and put everything down. He removed each mailing label from every piece of mail or magazine. He told me that suppose someone littered and his paper was in the bag of garbage, that junk mail or magazine could be attributed to him and perhaps he would be fined. Jack also said people could see a lot of his magazines and junk mail and build a "profile" of him if the mailing labels were on it. I think Jack had the first shredder I ever saw and shredded the mailing labels.

Jack was also one of the first people I knew to have a tape recorder cassette answering machine. He always said this is 23456 instead of Jack. He told me that was the way to go because people could cold call numbers and collect information such as a name and telephone number. If he was not there, it was only necessary to give the number and if the caller was legitimate, they knew they had the correct phone number and would leave a message. It seemed to make sense. Over twenty years later I see people commonly employing these techniques and calling it information security.

21.1.1 – The Credit Card

I was talking to someone who said it was easy to find out someone's mother's name through some of these genealogy websites. They said that perhaps if they had a credit card number that they could use the mother's maiden name and the credit card number to do identity theft. The person told me that waiters or waitresses will often go around the corner with your credit card to the machine to run it through while your still sitting in at the restaurant. Some will also use the cell phone with the camera to take a picture of the front and back of the card once they are around the corner and out of sight. They have your 3 digit security code on the back, the number, the expiration numbers, and the number to call the credit card number. The pictures of the cards can even be emailed as attachments to temporary accounts and deleted. It is therefore necessary to give your card only to people you trust or businesses you trust and the card should be processed in your sight. This fellow said that for security purposes, he told them his mother's maiden name was Rumpellstillskin with two sets of double Ls. He instructed his credit card company to always ask for the name and spelling. I said he was a smart fellow.

21.1.2 – Phishing

I also knew a fellow who got an email saying "dear valued PayPal Customer." He was suspicious because he cancelled his account two weeks earlier. The email asked him to click on the link and fill in the information. When he put the cursor on the link he was asked to click on, it gave a set of four numbers. Then he went to www.samespade.org and put it in a block and clicked on "do stuff." He found out the name, address, phone number, and tons of other information you could not believe. The website was registered in Shanghai. The fellow called PayPal and they said they have no website in China. They also never address people as dear valued customer, they always address you by your first name. I said that was an interesting story.

21.1.3 – Cell Phones, Mobile People, and Emergency Management

I was at a store and one of my senior citizen relatives was talking to this salesman. He was a real smooth talker and very personable. I imagined he made a lot of sales and excelled in his business. Many senior citizens I know seem to value people highly, enjoy small talk, and seem to like to learn things from conversing with local people much more than young folks do. The salesman got a cell phone call and took care of it quickly. He then went on to tell us he was a "floater", which means he works at a variety of stores as needed. He said he also stays with his brother, or other relatives or occasionally rents a place and does not want to share a phone. We got the impression he does not really have a permanent home. He had a cell phone because it is a way people can always reach him regardless of work or living accommodation.

It seemed fascinating that people use the cell phone instead of having an established land line in their house. He told us that this is a trend among many senior citizens as well as 20 somethings use because it is cheaper than a regular phone and he gets hours of long distance in his plan. He told me the senior citizens like it because they cannot always get up to answer a phone before it stops ringing. I said that was smart and excellent for elderly people for both accessibility and saving money. He said he saw no downside. He said he never got bothered by any telemarketers either. He did not give out the number and telemarketers call a local area code, a local exchange, and numbers from 0000 to 9999 and if you are not in between you are not bothered. They use call centers and predictive dialers.

There was a downside. I mentioned that suppose he lived near Route 287 in Morristown and a pesticide truck overturned and a pesticide was released in the air. The police station could not use the local reverse 911 to call you and let you know of the emergency route and that something happened. When an accident such as a pesticide spills, a first responder such as the New Jersey State Police secures the area and would use the incident command system. The state police at that site would be the Incident Commander since he is the first responder and interstate highways are the domain of the state police. Most likely the State Police Emergency Operations Center (EOC) would get their GIS (Geographical Information Service) fellow to pinpoint the accident on the map using ESRI ArcGIS and get the data from the weather website. A plume would be mapped and the map would be frequently updated as the weather conditions would change minute by minute. The moving plume would be mapped and tracked. Everyone in the affected areas would be notified by reverse 911. Thousands of calls can be made per hour with a recorded message. Such a message can tell you whether to shelter in place at home or to take an evacuation route.

Sometimes it is better to shelter in place and put up plastic on the windows and duct tape them. Then depending on the heaviness of the chemical plume and the wind, the instructions may be to go to a high point or a low point in your building. It is often said to have precut pieces of plastic for each window and duct tape around because you do not get much time in an emergency. The man said he never considered an emergency but said if he saw a panic he would call a neighbor to see what is going on and listen to the local AM radio.

21.1.4 – Data Casting

I had some great aunts who have since passed on since they were nearly 100 years old, but they once had a house within sight of the Oyster Creek Nuclear Plant in New Jersey. I was told that the plant often released millions of gallons of hot water in the local stream by my aunt's house and some of the people fishing on the trestle by the nuclear plant told me the hot water drifted in the current down to Florida and you could catch some fish common to Florida there along with local fish. I was told by some of the locals that swimming was also possible in cold weather too due to the release of large volumes of warm water on a regular basis. I expressed concern about living so close to a nuclear plant in case of an emergency but everyone told me they were a good responsible neighbor.

That good neighborliness has continued as New Jersey Network Public Television, the State Police Office of Emergency Management, OEM, had a drill to send emergency data along the TV network on March 4, 2003. When you and I watch New Jersey Network TV, we see a lot of educational programs and programs about community events and even some British Broadcasting Corporation (BBC) News. However; part of the signal is not used for TV but is used for sending text data to specially equipped computers. This concept could be compared to the main AM carrier and sideband in radio. Data casting is the practice of using a main carrier for a purpose such as a TV signal and then using a small bandwidth for sending text to computers on digital television signals.

The drill connected the computers of the New Jersey State Police NJSP Office of Emergency Management OEM in West Trenton, New Jersey with the Triveni Digital Skyscraper, and office of emergency management offices in the EPZ, Emergency Planning Zone around the Oyster Creek Nuclear Plant. The drill was a success and the shared data added to the overall preparedness of the area. It was upsetting to all of us here in New Jersey when we heard that drawings of Oyster Creek Nuclear plant were found in caves in Afghanistan, after 9/11. The area around the nuclear plant had large populations of retired people and young families who just want to have a nice life and not bother anyone. I can think of all the nice people around my great aunt's house. Why would anyone wish old people and young families harm?

21.2 – Citizen's Band Radio Network

There was a time in the mid 70s when the citizen's band radio functioned much like the Internet does today except on a very local level. There were people who would get on there and "jaw" talk about all kinds of political topics and others would use it to make blind dates much like these personal dating sites today except on a really small scale. The citizens band radio, commonly called a "CB" was a public forum for expressing ideas and being social for a subset of the town's population. You could hear senior citizens, kids, teenagers, and truckers. The CB was made famous by the movie "Convoy." Other movies like "Smokey and The Bandit" with Sally Fields and Burt Reynolds added to the CB craze.

The CB did have a serious side that promoted security and emergency management. Channel 9 was monitored by the police and people where I lived used it responsibly like 911. It was used to report fires, disabled vehicles, and other emergencies such as heart attacks. Sometimes tow trucks would monitor the frequencies and assist disabled vehicles or help the elderly change a tire. It was an effective emergency network.

Channel 19 was for talking on the highway and getting directions when you were lost. People did not have cell phones or global positioning systems (GPS) where you type in the location and it gives you all the verbal instructions of lefts and rights that you need to get to your location. My grandfather, who was a trucker, said that the most knowledgeable people on the road and the best drivers were truckers. I consider him a subject matter expert on trucking.

He said it was great to ask them how to get anywhere. The CB still exists today. You had to have a CB license back then but not today. The license had to be displayed by the station. My father's name was misspelled on the license and he got junk mail after that for 20 years with that misspelled name. I thought of "Jack" and how he tracked where information went.

Citizen's band was limited to five watts of power which was fine for local communication. If you had a 3 db gain antenna, that was like putting out 6 watts. Each 3 decibels gain has the same effect as if you doubled your power. That is why it is important to check the gain of an antenna. Some people had linear amplifiers that took power from the outlet and merged it with the signal out to create an illegal strong signal that drowned out other people. Some people would purposely "step on others" or drown them out if they did not like their views for example. The same concept is used on a large scale when countries have killer satellites to knock out other countries satellites when they broadcast certain types of propaganda messages and illicit programming.

CB radios started with 23 channels, then went up to 40, then with upper and lower sidebands. Remember the main signal and the side carriers? Are you thinking of data casting? The CB was another type of network tool that could be used in the car or home and performed as a medium for security tasks before the cell phone and personal computers were available to the masses.

21.3 – Lost Cell Phones

Recently a staff member picked up a phone at my workplace and asked how we find the owner. I said here is the number on the phone, so let us go to the website www.freeality.com and do a reverse lookup on the cell phone number. She did that and thought it was cool. Then we wanted to get the phone to the owner as soon as possible. I said it would take a while if we mail it to the person on the reverse lookup. Then I suggested going in the cell phone's last number called option and dialing it up.

The person who answered the phone number I dialed thought I was his mom. He must have had caller ID. I explained that the phone was lost, where the staff member was located, the staff member's phone number, and other point of contact details. The young man would have his older brother pick it up that day before the office closed.

21.3.1 – Cell Phone (I.C.E)(In Case of Emergency)

According to the Neighbor News, English ambulance service paramedic Bob Brotchie launched "ICE [1]." Many people have no information about finding the next of kin. It makes it easy to find out about blood types, allergies, etc.. if an unconscious person has an ICE contact in the Cell Phone. Ice is an acronym for in case of emergency and should have name and contact information for the next of kin. It is encouraged for everyone to tell others to put in ICE in their cell phones.

We know there were some horrid bombings in London on July 7th, 2005 where 56 people were killed and many others were injured. Some of the survivors did make contact with loved ones quickly, thanks to mobile phone technology. In the case of those slain it is important to be able to contact a family member too because there can be religious considerations such as the person must be buried by sunset.

21.3.2 – The Information Technology Professional and the Ego

Some people have such a big ego it is amazing. In the 1980s, I remember exercising at a gym and all these amateur body builders would exercise in front of the mirror. They would constantly talk about definition, pose, and fish for compliments from people who would notice increased muscle size or the appearance of a new vein. I believe a famous psychologist named Piaget says we go through five phases in our lives and one phase includes a time where people are really into looking good and exercising. However; I thought the inflated ego went too far when one of the body builders made a remark and kissed his bicep.

Many people in private industry have told me that they have met people in information technology who are very creative and find innovative solutions to problems. However; there exists a perception sometimes among corporate professionals that many information technology professionals do not seem to find adequate recognition of their achievements in the workplace. I am not a psychologist and cannot make a professional assessment but it is my personal opinion that the gap between one's perceived self worth and actual recognition could be from an inflated ego. Perhaps sometimes this ego can surface at places outside the workplace such as conferences, parties, and in the pub, saloon, or bar. The problem is when the person with the ego seeks recognition from a lay person outside of work they could, unwittingly, be talking to a competitor who through flattery might use certain information improperly or even illegally.

I was at a computer conference in 2000 in Seattle where Bill Gates spoke. The hotel had a pub and many people invited me for a drink. Conference attendees mixed freely with academics, corporate IT types, and government people. Other guests from the hotel who knew about the conference but had nothing to do with it could go to the pub and mix with conference attendees. One memory from the conference was recently jarred by an article I saw again when I was cleaning up conference memorabilia on my bookshelves and photo albums. I will first relate the incident and then discuss the article. I was standing with my Ph.D. mentor and some of the bright young men from English Universities getting super jobs with Intel and Microsoft. I noticed that there was an unusually attractive young woman with a nerdy man who was drawing a diagram on what appeared to be a napkin. The woman appeared unusually interested in what the man said and what he drew but her facial expressions and body language, including distance, did not appear to correspond to her level of interest. She did not seem to like him in my opinion.

Recently I had read that sometimes people will go to a high tech conference or a bar in a city and talk to nerdy technology people to learn about new products in development or the topology of a corporate network. Some of the information technology professionals are creative types whose ego is not satisfied by the level of recognition they receive and their high salary is not satisfying the need for praise and recognition for their efforts. A man or woman may approach the person who looks like a nerdy technology type and then feed that person drinks and compliments to find out company strategies, new products, and a network topology. I could imagine that a sufficiently inebriated man may even want to show off to a women and brag about a possible backdoor he or she put in a network to fix things remotely.

Suppose that man in the last example is married and an affair results in a preplanned location and is recorded. It is possible the man may be contacted and later blackmailed and recruited to become a corporate spy rather than have the affair made public or knowledge of his unprofessional conduct be revealed to his office or his spouse. It is my lay opinion that a company or organization that deals in trade secrets and proprietary knowledge needs to have an active human resources department that has non disclosure and non compete policies signed as well as other policies, signed, dated and filed. A security training program warning of travel problems is probably a good idea. Such topics can include information security like using public computers and then clearing the forms and passwords. It can be simple things such as hanging up the laptop on the hook inside the door when using the toilet. It can be using a privacy hood when doing work on the laptop on the screen in a public area. Other topics can be talking to people interested in your work, revealing information on the skyphone in a quiet place like in your airline seat. Sensitive discussions about alcohol and "skirt chasing" may be included.

21.3.3 – Extraction Team

There are some organizations that sell mainframes and personal computers from corporation or government entities from one country to another. I was once interviewed for a job a few years ago that wanted me for my mainframe and PC experience, but I chose not to take it. A fellow once said that he had a team that removed a mainframe and all peripherals from Manhattan and then packaged everything up and sold it to a buyer in Bogota, Columbia. I learned in the last six months that such business is complicated and everything has to be wiped clean, certified as sanitized, and there has to be an export license. I know today that the United States Commerce Department also has a list of technology that can and cannot be exported. There is a lot of kidnapping in Columbia because members of organized crime sometimes block the road with fake checkpoints to kidnap people. This seems to be such a common practice that companies will even take out kidnapping insurance for their technology employees and corporate executives who visit questionable locations.

There are even private security companies who have or can contract with others to organize an extraction team. These are teams that are similar to civilian search and rescue teams. Suppose a few people go to a country on the south of the Saudi Peninsula and set up a mainframe and do some computer training work and a security concern arises. That person's security plan was to call Mr. X. who would meet them and they would speed to the docks in a jeep. Once Mr. X meets the computer professionals, the extraction team in a helicopter is notified and they may take a stealth boat across the Arabian Sea to a predetermined site such as a small island off Somalia. The speed of the boat and its location could be tracked by the extraction team using a global positioning system. An extraction team of lightly armed men in a helicopter could arrive about the same time as the boat. The lightly armed men could be to fight off any resistance from any pursuing motor boats or gun boats. The helicopter might lower a harness to rescue the team since landing may not be possible. This is one example of a privately contracted extraction team might operate.

We can see an example of a military extraction team in the movie "Black Hawk Down" which is based on a true story. There is a man who drives a car with a big X duct taped on top of the car. He is visible from the air to the crews in the helicopter. He does not have a global positioning device (GPS). Then he parks in front of the hotel where the warlord is. He opens the hood and fakes car trouble which is the signal for the building with the warlord. The helicopters are then dispatched to that spot and armed men are lowered to the site to get the prisoners. That is an example of how a well orchestrated military extraction team operates.

When I lived in the urban Midwest going to college there was a white vehicle at the gas station that was about 50% of the size of the M48 Sherman tank. The white vehicle was solid and had a large bore gun on the front. I put my hand on the vehicle and asked the gas station owner what it was for. He told me it was used by the police to get into dangerous areas and extract an armed threat in the community. He said it was called an urban assault vehicle.

21.4 – Wireless Security Techniques to Prevent Terrorism

We see that the plan in the movie "Black Hawk Down" did not go as expected because some of the people on the warlord's side had a telecommunication network and a visual network for a backup. The telecommunication network was a cell phone network. Now we know from reading in the newspapers that terrorists will use cell phones with a bomb and call the number. When the cell phone next to the bomb rings, it activates a switch and goes off. One strategy they use in Israel to prevent simultaneous bombs going off is to flood the cell phone networks with electronic packets so it is jammed and no further calls and signals for bombs can occur.

Based on what I saw in the movie "Black Hawk down", it is my opinion that the warlord in Mogadishu was a well informed man because he must have anticipated that cell phones could be jammed and not relied on extensively. He then had people burn tires which formed a smoke cloud and signaled people which way the helicopter attack came from. This low tech method was not only a backup but served as a communication method for people without cell phones. You would think that helicopters make a lot of noise and everyone would hear them but they are quiet. In college I was living in an urban Midwest environment and weeding a vegetable garden when a police helicopter and sniper flew overhead. I never heard it coming until it was directly overhead. I heard later by people in the neighborhood that a police officer was pinned down some blocks away by drug dealers with AK47s and the helicopter was used to save his life. I was told too that flying low reduces all the noise.

21.5 – Wireless Security

There are some things we can do to increase wireless security. Suppose you have a Linksys Wireless Router Switch as in figure 21.1. Then you can access it through the browser by going to 192.168.1.1 and then use the set up page there to register. You would probably want to first change the local IP address to something that hackers would find only after a long time of scanning such as 245.168.1.1 and by then they might move on to someone else. You can also change the password to something with capital and small letters as well as letters and numbers. This will make a dictionary attack nearly impossible. The idea is to make your system just a pain to break into so that it is best for the hacker to move on to an easier target. You probably will not stop a determined hacker with sophisticated tools and loads of time, but you are probably not the Pentagon either, so they will move to find a softer target.

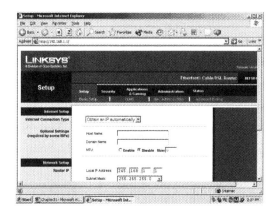

Figure 21.1 – The Linksys Router Switch

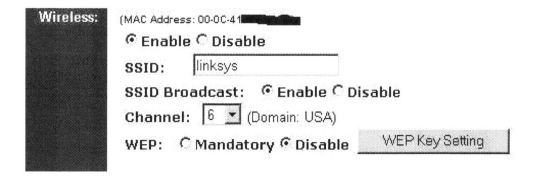

Figure 21.2 – Channels and Wireless Equivalent Protocol

There are six channels on the Linksys router / switch. Sometimes people have various wireless devices like cordless phones, wireless cameras, and other devices where there is interference so they can change the channel. However it is better to change the default so people riding around slowly in your neighborhood in the car with a laptop and wireless card do not easily connect to your network. Such people are called "war drivers" and will mark the street in front of your house indicating wireless access and the speed. Some people I know thought that these marks in the street were made by the water department, the sewer authority, or the electric company.

There is a whole underground community with markings for wireless connectivity. In the 1930s my grandmother had many beggars ring the doorbell for a sandwich and coffee. She lived near the railroad and noticed other houses nearby did not get so many beggars ringing the bell. She was doing some work outdoors and found some markings in chalk and erased them. Then the visits stopped. Many years later it was said people in the 1930s called hobos would jump on and off trains during the "Great Depression" and get off in various parts of the country and seek food, drink, and temporary jobs. They had their own language which was expressed in markings on various buildings. This system of markings can be seen in the movie called "Emperor of the North Pole" with Lee Marvin.

Recently I was talking to a policeman who was an expert on gangs. We took a class together on a security related topic. The classroom that we were in was leased for the class. He pointed out gang markings in our class room that were from members of three prominent street gangs. I was in the room and was unaware of them until he pointed them out. He also told me other things in the neighborhood that were marked. He was right and that is why he is the trained observer and security professional.

When it comes to having the Service Set Identifier (SSID) enabled and broadcasting, anyone with a laptop and wireless card knows right away if it is Linksys so change it to another name. There are common names of networks that tell people it is a piece of Cisco, Linksys, or other type of equipment. If they know the type of equipment you have, they can read up on it, get applets from the Internet, and possibly compromise your security. It is also important to enable the Wireless Equivalent Privacy (WEP) key and put in a phrase that will generate a set of keys based on the ASCII code for the number. Captial A is 41 and small A is 64. You can get the ASCII chart from many places on the Internet. The phrase and keys generated can be seen in figure 21.3 below.

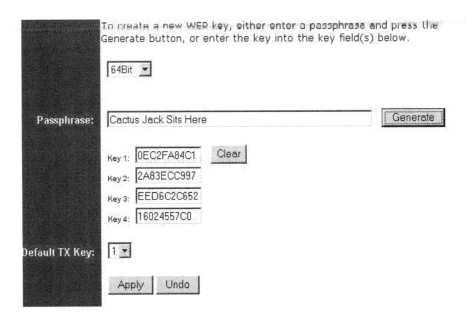

Figure 21.3 WEP Passphrase and Keys

21.6 – The Wireless / Radio Controlled Planes

In the late 1990s I was working on my doctorate in England and teaching as an adjunct professor in the United States between trips to England. I taught introduction to computers class and there were some computer geniuses in the class but they took it to establish a paper trail of their knowledge. Sometimes people are self taught or learn things at work but have no way to document their knowledge. There was a young man in my class who was really brilliant. He told me he was a ham radio or amateur radio operator. He got into the hobby because he liked radio controlled airplanes and ham radio allowed him to use frequencies and high power that permitted him to fly radio controlled planes at very high altitudes and for quite considerable distances. He also used a laptop and wireless camera and would go to a remote location and fly the plane up to a half mile high and get the aerial video feed on the laptop. He talked about this field by a swamp in an industrial center too which I happened to pass one day. People were flying helicopters and practicing maneuvers such as making precise landings, hovering low to the ground, and it looked like it was a serious and expensive hobby.

I talked to the young man at the end of the class and he told me that he was a biologist and had an interest in environmental sciences. He said the radio controlled aircraft with video allowed him to fly to remote locations that were inaccessible to him to collect data. At the time it seemed a little odd but working part time as a computer consultant at the company that directed toxic waste cleanup and did explosion investigation, I had been thinking how some areas are difficult to get samples from safely. My young boss who died of a neurological disorder, told me stories about nasty places he helped clean up where smoke went into the atmosphere and reacted with chemicals and came down and had made six inches of a fiberglass like material on the ground. At the time, I assumed the young man was talking about checking very polluted or radioactive places and dismissed it.

While writing this book that memory had surfaced and I thought the young man had his own version of an unmanned aerial vehicle (UAV). Security professionals need to add UAV into their security plan because they are easy to get and equip with cameras, video cameras, air quality sensors, and possibly other kinds of sensors. They could deliver a payload of some sort or even be used to gather intelligence. Perhaps if a security professional at a high security facility used a scanner in the 6 meter band and 27 Megahertz band and then if a strong control signal appeared s/he would know that was the control frequency. Then if s/he had a very strong signal and a radio controller, the security professional could actually take over the remote controlled aircraft and land it thus removing any threat.

21.7 – Wireless Clocks that Synchronize with the Atomic Clock

It is a problem when we do not know the correct time or if our clock is wrong. We can be late for work, appointments, and countless other problems. There is a clock that I bought known as the Wyeth Wall Clock with Atomic Time. The clock documentation recommends it is to be put by the window and away from other electronic equipment. There are buttons for many time zones. You can put in the battery and push the button and the clock will synchronize wirelessly with the atomic clock and self adjust for daylight savings time and even leap seconds.

21.8 – Conclusion

It is important to change the default settings on any wireless equipment and read about your wireless equipment to see what changes you should make. It is also important to use an intrusion detection system and firewall to see when people have broken in your system and to also keep unauthorized people out. It is also important to use common sense when dealing with others and realize you are vulnerable when traveling and staying in a hotel and using public computers to check email. It is important to clear forms, clear passwords, and talk to computer security professionals before going on a trip and learn what and what not to do.

REFERENCES

1. "Cell Phone Can Provide Emergency Information", Published at 100 Commons Way, Rockaway, New Jersey, 07866-116, Page 24, August 10,2005, Phone 973-586-8190

Chapter 22 –
The End of the Book

22.1 – Introduction

If you have made it this far, you can see by my full name, Eamon Doherty that I have an ancestry from the "Emerald Isle" and am a bit of a story teller. I come from a long line of people that enjoyed telling a story, playing cards, and reading books. On the serious side, I have a lot of Irish American relatives who have served as chaplains to the fire service or risked their lives as volunteer fireman to save children, the elderly, and the disabled. We are going to finish the book with two stories that have to do with networks, card playing, and the fire service. The first is a story about historic card cheats and modern international card playing cheats and its detriment to online casinos. The second story is about some of the technology and networks to support the brave men and women of the fire services.

22.2 Introduction to Historic Problems in Card Playing

When I was quite young there seemed to be a lot more interest in playing cards then there is today. There were many people who got together to play bridge, cribbage, or canasta. Perhaps it was that people had more free time and did not have to commute so far or sit in traffic. This friendly social part of card playing still exists in my opinion but not to the level it once did.

Card playing also has its uglier side too. My grandfather Doherty, who was born in 1889 and who has long since passed away, told stories about a candy store that existed in his urban neighborhood that had the same pieces of hard candy for sale year after year in a small store front and was known for a poker game and other card games in a secret room in the back. There was supposedly a spot where you would stand and a small panel was actually a revolving door to the back room. It was said that some of the people who went there worked in teams to cheat at cards by having non verbal signals to discuss what cards were needed and what they had. They would sit in certain places where it was possible to pass a team member a card through discarding. Touching a glass, or parts of one's face could indicate a suit, and a nervous drum of the fingers might be counted to indicate a number card. Teamwork might be obvious if one person discards a pair of queens and the person next to him or her picks it up. The honest player by himself did not stand a chance of winning big.

22.2.1 – Card Playing Troubles in the Casino Today

There was a show recently on cable television that said casinos still experience teams of people with a system of non verbal communication working together to unfairly beat the odds. However; there is a network of video cameras that are monitored in the casino by security professionals upstairs and suspicious behavior can be disrupted by a "pit boss" who walks around the floor supervising games. S/he usually has what appears to be a hearing aid but is usually part of a wireless network that keeps physical security, the monitoring team, and pit boss connected and working as a team to keep gambling honest. Once some cheats are identified, their facial characteristics are recorded through biometrics that can be used to identify such people and may play a part in keeping them from entering the casino later.

22.2.2 – Card Playing Troubles on Online Casinos

There was an article in Security Management magazine that discussed some problems in online gambling [1]. It seems that historic problems such as teams working together to cheat, first manifest themselves in some informal gathers such as the one my grandfather spoke of, then manifest themselves at modern casinos, and finally at online casinos. It seems that the same old "offenses" manifest themselves every time a new medium develops.

I was told by a historian that investment schemes known as pyramid schemes have existed for thousands of years and now appear on the Internet too. You can pay ten dollars to join this society and then each person who joins gives you five dollars and perhaps the person who recruited you five dollars. The tree expands at an exponential rate and soon cannot sustain the rate of growth it needs to continue and fails. This is another example of the same old crime that appears every time a new medium appears.

There was a website that allowed people to do online gambling fairly anonymously where accounts and credit cards could be used for both putting money in an account and winners could get money back in the form of a chargeback. The website also allowed for money to be sent by wire where it could be quickly obtained, an account cancelled, and all transactions were done quickly and efficiently. This is great for people who want to play, but is bad for the casinos if international cheats work the system.

The website had a problem when many people were online using the same account and it looked like one player when it was actually several. There were also times when groups of players around the world joined a card game and appeared to be strangers but actually worked together by supplying each other with cards through discards that the other needed. Perhaps they were on cell phones or used less traceable means of communicating such as the videoconference package called "Netmeeting." It was obvious if a person through down a pair of queens or kings and another person at the table picked them up.

22.23 – International Crime

It was even worse when people used stolen credit cards for an account and were playing with other's money. Perhaps one might even be using as many as 100 credit cards in a variety of accounts and the card numbers may not have even been reported stolen. There may also be no indicators of previous gambling if there were no history of charge backs. People could quickly create online accounts, use stolen credit cards to gamble, work in teams, and have the money wired to a place that might be difficult to get extradition from. Then the accounts may be quickly dissolved and the players start again with new accounts. The wide distances across countries and the anonymity of the accounts made it difficult to prove "teams" and also made tracking criminal activities difficult. They needed a set of detectives to investigate the crimes because a casino may work on a small profit margin and such crime might put the casino out of business.

22.2.4 – Stopping the Online Crime

It may not be possible to successfully prosecute rings of international criminals but it is possible to stop them. The online casino hired poker experts and various security experts to examine card playing and IP addresses. The feasible solution to the problem seemed to be to reduce it to a level that the casino could live with by installing a security system called "ieSnare" that linked accounts with a physical location, ISP, and certain characteristics of the computer itself. It made it so the criminals would have to use a completely different ISP, machine, for each new account. The ieSnare system also has features that allow investigators a method to map relationships between accounts, machines, and players and thus identify cheating. This made it so inconvenient that the cheats probably went to a place where the "pickings" were easier.

22.2.5 – A Casino / Hotel / Restaurant for Casino Patrons and Crime

The restaurants that serve the casino patrons also experience crimes by its employees. The employees may bring extra coupons and then apply them when a patron did not. This would allow them to pocket the savings and it would not appear stealing occurred. Some friends or others who prearranged a deal may not be "rung up" which is an inappropriate comp. Comp is an abbreviation for compensation that is given to casino patrons or staff. One place was able to apply a system called Smart Connect on a large scale. The new security system to stop some of the cheating and inappropriate comps cost US$366,000.00 to implement and saves between US$110,000 - US$186,000 per year. The casino hotel owners say the system will pay for itself in two to three years. The other good side is that such a system allows security personnel to work more efficiently

22.3 – Fire Service Communication

In my grandfather's time, there were fire service men with leather buckets that formed a bucket brigade. Communication was done by passing buckets and a verbal message. Then later there were wagons with horses. These wagons had a long bar for three men to pump. This allowed pressure to form and a man with a hose could then fight the fire. Shouting, hand signals, and a megaphone were ways that could be used for communication from chiefs to the person spraying the fire.

Today radios are used but sometimes environments exist that are so noisy that shouting cannot be heard inches away. To solve the problems of communicating in noisy environments, there are skull microphones that pick up vibrations resonating in bones from speaking. Fire service personnel also use a small monocle that is mounted on a helmet and is placed approximately one inch from the firefighter's eye. This monocle is an organic light emitting diode made by eMagin that gives the illusion of seeing a nine by twelve foot screen. This monocle can be connected to a portable computer system that allows maps of the building and other pertinent information to appear to aid the fire fighter. The system can also be coupled with a thermal camera system to allow the fire fighter to see a child hiding in the corner of a burning building in complete darkness.

REFERENCES

1. Longmore-Etheridge, A., (2005),"Deal Fraud Out", Security Management by ASIS International, September 2005
2. " ", Pages 47-48

Chapter 23 –
Powerful Storms and Networks

23.1 – Introduction to Storms and Networks
This chapter is an important afterthought which came about because of the terrible storm Katrina that has caused so much death, sickness, and destruction of property in the New Orleans area. We will discuss a variety of networks and how they play out in improving the lives of people affected by this storm in the summer of 2005.

23.1.1 – A Personal Story of Storms and Networks
You only have to turn on the television to see the good and bad sides of people reacting to the terrible storm Katrina that sent high winds and a wall of water through the City of New Orleans in Louisiana. A satellite collected data about a storm moving through the Gulf of Mexico and toward the southern states of the United States. The data was sent to the ground and linked to the Internet to a Geographical Information System (GIS) through "Google Earth" See www.earth.google.com. The results of such a system allowed members of the public who could connect to the Internet to see a map of the ongoing storm as well as its speed and direction. Similar maps were displayed on television during the news to inform citizens who did not have personal computers with Internet access.

The local government in New Orleans took a bidirectional road and temporarily made it one way to allow for the maximum throughput of vehicles out of town. Many people saw the weather maps and GIS systems on the Internet and decided the best plan of action was evacuation. They filled their vehicles with valuables and supplies and left. Others who could not afford their own vehicle rented one and left. Others took the train or bus. Many people did not believe the storm would be that bad and felt the mapped data was inaccurate and stayed behind. Television gives the impression that many poor people and the elderly could not leave and if they did perhaps had no place to go.

A person from New Jersey, who will be known hereafter as Bob, moved to New Orleans evacuated to Mississippi. There was no cell phone coverage where he was. It was some time until he could arrange transportation from where he was to a location where cell phone coverage was possible. Many people had the same idea as he did and the network was flooded with packets. It was a day later when he was able to contact relatives in my community. He then made his way back to the area where many of the refugees of the flood were staying. The phone call he made was brief and he was lucky to get through.

Bob's nephew stayed in his house while the flood raged on from water from Lake Pochatrain and the local levees. The nephew had plenty of food and water in the bathtub on the second floor. The water reached the second floor after a few days. There was no electricity, cell phone service, clean running water, TV, or telephone service. The man was isolated and uninformed. He decided to swim to the elevated interstate highway where he climbed on and was rescued. The nephew was flown to a place where he could get medical attention after swimming through water that was filled with sewage. He also told authorities he saw what appeared to be unconscious or deceased people some distance away when he was on the bridge.

Bob was able to locate his wife at the refugee center and they made their way north to the New York / New Jersey metropolitan area where their relatives own a vacation home. Bob got a call on his cell phone from a neighbor who was at the refugee center. Bob said his neighbor was able to get to a mobile command vehicle which had some Internet Access and use a GIS system to get a satellite photo of their neighborhood. The satellite photo had information about the streets and it was possible to keep clicking to closer view. They could see flooding but the houses were intact. This was a relief. Many people in other parts of Louisiana and Alabama had lost their homes. GIS allowed a person to see an area and zoom in on it. Maybe you would like to do a Google Earth search on satellite maps showing where you live. Perhaps you could locate a GIS system available with your property. I was once practicing using GIS while taking a class and was able to zoom in on a place in San Francisco near where a friend of mine lived. The detail was so clear I could see one house had what looked like a ramp for wheelchair access.

I gave Bob's mom an extra computer, cable modem, and fax, color printer / color copier from my basement. She was able to get it to Bob who set it up. Bob's mom's vacation home had cable television and he was able to call the cable company and have Internet access added. Bob then could telecommute to his employer in Louisiana which had branches all over the USA and collect email and conduct business in his area. The fax would also allow him to send and receive documents that were not convenient to scan and email. Bob was able to resume his business for an oil company on a limited scale from the vacation home for some months until he and his wife could return home.

23.2 – The Network of the Red Cross

The Red Cross is an organization that provides international relief from disasters to people around the world. A neighbor rented a giant truck and about a hundred local people brought wheelbarrows full of battery powered radios, clocks, shoes, blankets, tools, and clothing. The neighbor's sister was a relief volunteer for the Red Cross and drove to Mississippi to help flood victims. The most helpful item in my opinion was a flashlight and radio that worked for approximately a half hour with a couple revolutions of the handle. The device did not need batteries. Another person had a flashlight that you just shake left and right with moderate force. The flashlight has a weight that rides on a track and works in unison with a dynamo to generate electricity for the flashlight. No batteries are needed.

Another man I knew was a senior citizen named Artie. He ran classes to train a hundred New Jersey people who wanted to be Red Cross volunteers, in two weeks. After he ran the classes, he was going to areas where Katrina hit to help feed 1500 people a day with two types of meals. The first type of meal is provided by the National Guard and is known as an MRE, meal ready to eat. The second type of meal is the Heater Meal. These meals have a tray and a sponge underneath. One you wet the sponge, a reaction occurs and the meal is heated. Artie says some people tell him the heater meals have more variety and taste better than the MRE.

23.3 – Amateur Radio and Disasters (ARES)

The amateur radio operator will often have a set of radios that work on HF, high frequency, VHF very high frequency, and SHF, super high frequency. The amateur radio operator is not paid for his or her service and will often volunteer to help with communications in such disaster situations. These operators often have a phone patch similar to the one shown in figure 23.1. The phone patch allows two people connected by a radio to access a phone line. Then the people on the radio and the person on the phone can all communicate on a half duplex method. That means one person talks while the other listens. The person says 'over' to indicate s/he is finished speaking temporarily. The idea of the phone patch is not to avoid long distance charges but facilitate emergency communication. The whole conversation is also transmitted on the airwaves and can be picked up by anyone with a good antenna, receiver, and in the path of the propagated waves.

Many amateur radio operators will take a car battery and use it as temporary power since most radios have an option for twelve volts. Some amateur radio operators connect a solar panel to batteries to keep them charged. Others will use an alternator connected to a homemade windmill for power. Many years ago, I once saw a man that had a generator connected to his bike by rubbing against the wheel. He would pedal and talk on the radio.

Some radios can be connected to a terminal node controller (TNC) and used with a laptop which also is battery powered. This allows for a packet station and can be used to send text messages for health and welfare. Many people who wish to help in such disasters join a group called ARES which is an acronym for the Amateur Radio Emergency Service.

23.3.1 – Radio Amateur Civil Emergency Service (R.A.C.E.S.)

Sometimes there are events besides floods and disasters, where volunteers will provide digital and radio communication. There are often annual events such as New Years Eve party or St. Patrick's Day Parade where there are a lot of people who could have a problem and be in need first aid. Since 9-11 has occurred, RACES members may also be watching for suspicious behavior indicating terrorism. At such events there is often a collaboration of the Civil Air Patrol, RACES, the ambulance squad, the firemen, and the police. All volunteers and first responders will be given radios if they do not have one. They will all be assigned zones and some may have cell phones as a backup or for private communication. There will be a command frequency for the police and those running the event too. A tactical frequency will be common among everyone for the small details of carrying out events. Quite often, a first aid event will occur and then the rescue squad is informed. Once they take over the situation and have responsibility, they will take it offline to their rescue squad command and tactical frequencies so the big radio network is free for other situations. Members must be taught to keep radio silence unless a situation occurs and radio silence means teamwork. People need to work as a team for it to succeed.

Figure 23.1 – Yaesu Radio and Phone Patch

There is an event where ARES, RACES, and various other amateur radio clubs practice emergency communication outdoors all across the United States. This event often has thousands or tens of thousands of people participating. It is called field day and happens every June in the United States. People work as many stations as possible on each band with various modes such as a computer; microphone and telegraph key and then mark a map with the results. This will show them what frequencies and modes of communication can best reach an area in a real emergency.

23.4 Future Work
We hope we have inspired you to help use communication to help the elderly, children, the disabled, and everyone needing assistance in emergencies. We have also discussed many technologies and techniques to use robotic arms to help people work. We have also discussed network security and computer investigations and we hope you learned things that you can use at work. We will soon write a book on emergency management and recovery methods.

23.5 – Thanks to My Dad
My father Edward Doherty had helped me for many years with the Satellite Dish, packet radios, phone patch, and with the Morse code until he passed away in 1997. He was also really proud

when I set up a teleconference between mission STS-83 Space Shuttle and hundreds of kids at the County College of Morris. I also learned a lot about telephones from my dad. My dad was a lineman and telephone expert in the Marine Corps in the 3rd Amphibious Corp in World War Two. He knew about network security because he was an Irish American equipment man / lineman assigned to work with the Navajo Code talkers at Guam and Guadalcanal. He said approximately 11 Native American languages and codes were also used in various American wars and the enemy never broke them. Nicholas Cage in the movie "Wind Talkers" made the Marines and Navajo Code Talkers famous."

Figure 23.2 – Ed Doherty on the Beach Guam after the Marines Secured the Island

www.ingramcontent.com/pod-product-compliance
Lightning Source LLC
Chambersburg PA
CBHW080412060326
40689CB00019B/4217